CITYSPOTS
LOND

Donna Dailey

Written by Donna Dailey
Original photography by Christopher Holt and Pictures Colour Library Ltd.
Front cover photography courtesy of Giovanni Simeone/4cornersimages.com
Series design based on an original concept by Studio 183 Limited

Produced by Cambridge Publishing Management
Project Editor: Tim Ryder
Layout: Trevor Double
Maps: PC Graphics
Reproduced by permission of Ordnance Survey on behalf of HMSO. © Crown
Copyright 2006. All rights reserved. Ordnance Survey Licence number 100035725.
Transport map: © Transport for London

Published by Thomas Cook Publishing
A division of Thomas Cook Tour Operations Limited
Company Registration No. 1450464 England
PO Box 227, Unit 18, Coningsby Road
Peterborough PE3 8SB, United Kingdom
email: books@thomascook.com
www.thomascookpublishing.com
+ 44 (0) 1733 416477
ISBN-13: 978-184157-636-7
ISBN-10: 1-84157-636-0

First edition © 2006 Thomas Cook Publishing
Text © 2006 Thomas Cook Publishing
Maps © 2006 Thomas Cook Publishing
Series Editor: Kelly Anne Pipes
Project Editor: Ross Hilton
Production/DTP: Steven Collins

Printed and bound in Spain by GraphyCems

CONTENTS

SYMBOLS & ABBREVIATIONS

The following symbols are used throughout this book:

ⓐ address   **ⓣ** telephone   **ⓕ** fax   **ⓔ** email   **ⓦ** website address
ⓛ opening times   **ⓝ** public transport connections   **ⓘ** important

The following symbols are used on the maps:

ⓘ information office   ○ city
✈ airport   ○ large town
✚ hospital   ○ small town
ⓩ police station   ═ motorway
▣ bus station   ━ main road
▤ railway station   ━ minor road
Ⓜ metro   — railway
✝ cathedral
❶ numbers denote featured cafés & restaurants

Hotels and restaurants are graded by approximate price as follows:
£ budget   **££** mid-range   **£££** expensive

◗ *Keeping an 'eye' on London, from the South Bank*

Introduction

London is one of the world's great cities. Spreading along the banks of the River Thames, it has been the capital of the country since Roman times. With a population of over seven million, it is one of the largest cities in Europe, a hub of banking and business, food and fashion, politics and entertainment.

London may be the showcase for British history and culture, but it is also a city of great diversity, with a dynamic mix of residents and visitors from around the globe. Ethnic minorities make up around a third of the population, and more than 270 nationalities call London home. They have given the capital its vibrant blend of customs and cuisines.

Back in the 18th century, Dr Samuel Johnson famously wrote that '...in London there is all that life can afford.' That still holds true today. You can shop for designer clothes and luxury goods in smart West End stores, or hunt for bargains in the many markets around the capital. You can eat in curry houses, noodle bars and trendy cafés, or dine on elegant French, Asian or modern British cuisine. London has palaces, monuments and some of the world's finest museums containing a wealth of art and artefacts. London is also a magnet for the performing arts. Theatre, opera, classical music and dance in the city are world-class.

After dark, you can dance till dawn in the city's famous nightclubs, and hear live music every night of the week. But the pub is still the heart and soul of London nightlife, and many of the old 'boozers' are full of character (and characters). Balancing the urban landscape are hundreds of green parks, squares and gardens. There's something for everybody to love in London, a city that never fails to impress.

▶ The Houses of Parliament are best viewed from the Thames

When to go

SEASONS & CLIMATE

London is great to visit at any time of the year, as there is plenty to do and see, and most of its attractions are not weather-dependent. The city is always prettier in the sunshine, when the brick buildings and the residents alike seem brighter and more welcoming. Of course, with Britain's climate, sunshine is never guaranteed in London or anywhere else. It can rain frequently even in summer months, so come prepared with a waterproof jacket and umbrella.

Summer is a popular time for visitors, as temperatures are highest (on average 20–22°C) and the daylight hours at their longest. School holidays from mid-July to early September also increase the visitor volume. May and September–October are quieter and still have warm weather. December through to February are the coldest months (on average 6–7°C). Accommodation can be cheaper then and sightseeing less crowded, though shops will be crowded before and after Christmas.

London's climate is generally pretty temperate year-round. Apart from a few days in August, it rarely gets too hot, and though winters may feel chilly, it seldom drops below freezing and frost and snow are rare.

ANNUAL EVENTS

There's always something going on in London. Here are a few of the main festivals and events that take place each year, but do check with the tourist information office for a comprehensive calendar of events when you're planning your visit ⓦ www.visitlondon.com. Local media such as *Time Out* magazine and the *Evening Standard* are also good sources of information.

January
The **New Year's Day Parade** winds from Parliament Square up Whitehall, Trafalgar Square and Piccadilly to Berkeley Square, with floats, dancers and marching bands.

February
Chinese New Year Chinatown sees in the new year with dancing dragons, fireworks and celebrations around Gerrard Street (in late Jan some years). ⓦ www.chinatownchinese.com

March
St Patrick's Day Parade and Festival A parade, Irish music, dancing, arts and crafts mark this popular festival in central London.
ⓦ www.london.gov.uk

◖ *A quick pint after work*

April
London Marathon Some 35,000 runners take part in one of the biggest city marathons in the world, and thousands more spectators come to cheer them on. Ⓦ www.london-marathon.co.uk

May
Chelsea Flower Show A highlight of the gardening year, with fabulous floral displays at the Chelsea Royal Hospital; tickets go on sale in Nov. Ⓦ www.rhs.org.uk

June
Trooping the Colour The Queen's official birthday celebration, with a royal procession along the Mall, a military ceremony at Horse Guards Parade, an Air Force fly-past and gun salute.

June/July
City of London Festival A broad programme of music and cultural events takes place over a fortnight, both in and outside some of the City's most famous buildings. Ⓦ www.colf.org

July/Sept
BBC Sir Henry Wood Promenade Concerts The famous Proms concerts in the Royal Albert Hall range from classical to modern music, ending with the patriotic Last Night, where crowds gather in Hyde Park. Ⓦ www.bbc.co.uk/proms

August
Notting Hill Carnival Parades Costumes, live bands, sound systems and 1–2 million visitors makes this two-day festival at the end of August the biggest street party in Europe. Ⓦ www.lnhc.org.uk

September
Mayor's Thames Festival A weekend waterfest along the Thames between Blackfriars and Westminster bridges, with a lantern procession and fireworks on Sunday night. ⓦ www.thamesfestival.org

October
London Film Festival The country's biggest film festival showcases 150 new British and international films over a fortnight at the National Film Theatre and other venues. ⓦ www.lff.org.uk

November
Bonfire Night Fireworks, bonfires and the burning of an effigy of Guy Fawkes, who failed to blow up Parliament in 1605, take place in parks across London on and around 5 Nov.

Late November/December
Christmas Tree Lighting The lights decorating a huge Norwegian spruce, an annual gift from Norway, in Trafalgar Square are switched on by a celebrity, and more lights decorate London's shopping streets.

PUBLIC HOLIDAYS
New Year's Day 1 January
Good Friday 6 April 2007, 10 April 2008
Easter Monday 9 April 2007, 13 April 2008
Spring Bank Holiday first Monday in May
May Bank Holiday last Monday in May
August Bank Holiday last Monday in August
Christmas Day 25 December
Boxing Day 26 December

Europe's biggest street party

The steel bands are ringing. The sound systems are thumping. Everyone is dancing in the street at London's most famous event, the Notting Hill Carnival. It's been called Europe's biggest street party, and every August Bank Holiday – the last weekend in August – between one and two million people turn up to stroll the streets of Notting Hill. Flashy costumes, parades and non-stop music are all part of this West Indian spectacle. Only the Carnival in Rio is bigger.

London's Carnival was started by Trinidadian immigrants to help bring people together after Britain's first race riots took place in Notting Hill in the late 1950s. Since 1964, it has grown into a year-round activity, with 10,000 people working to create this huge celebration of culture.

Notting Hill isn't the only part of London to take to the streets. Chinatown sees in the Chinese New Year (late Jan–early Feb) with a Grand Parade and Children's Parade from Leicester Square to Trafalgar Square, where there are traditional lion and dragon dancers, music, acrobatics and more. There are fireworks displays at Leicester Square and festivities all day in Chinatown.

Baishaki Mela, the Bangla New Year Festival, takes place in May in and around Brick Lane. With colourful processions, music, dancing, events and a food fair, it is the premier Bengali celebration outside of Bangladesh.

▶ *The carnival arrives in Notting Hill*

History

When the Romans invaded Britain in the first century AD, they established a settlement on the banks of the Thames, called Londinium, which became a busy trading port. Located where the City stands today, they surrounded it with a defensive wall and also built the first London Bridge.

After the Romans left in the 5th century, the Saxons took over the city. In 1042 Edward the Confessor was crowned king and established his court upstream at Westminster, where he built a new palace and abbey. Shortly after his death, William the Conqueror of Normandy defeated the English forces at the Battle of Hastings. He became King William I and constructed the first defences at the Tower of London.

London prospered during medieval times as a great centre of trade. Thousands died in the Black Death of 1348, but London's population was around 50,000 when Henry VIII came to the throne in 1509. When the Pope refused to annul his marriage to his first wife, which had failed to produce a male heir, Henry split with Rome and declared himself the head of the Church of England, bringing sweeping change to London and the country. Under the reign (1558–1603) of Elizabeth I, English explorers sailed around the world and established colonies. The arts flourished, including Shakespeare's Globe Theatre.

Turmoil wracked London in the 17th century, with the failed Gunpowder Plot to blow up Parliament in 1605 followed by the outbreak of Civil War in 1642, which culminated in the execution of Charles I in 1649. Londoners rejoiced with the Restoration of the monarchy in 1660 under Charles II. Science and the arts, which had been suppressed under strict Puritan law, flourished once again. But two great tragedies struck the city. The Great Plague of 1665 killed between 80,000 and 100,000 people, followed by the Great Fire in 1666, which destroyed four-fifths of the medieval city. London was reconstructed in brick, and Sir Christopher Wren rebuilt St Paul's Cathedral and the city's churches.

London mushroomed in both size and population during the 18th century, but there was a great gulf between rich and poor. Handsome Georgian houses and fashionable shops were built in the West End and cultural institutions like the British Museum were established. Industrialisation in the 19th century brought more prosperity and even greater change to the city, as railways, sewers and the first Underground line were built.

At the turn of the 20th century Britain's empire was at its height, and between the wars London's population grew to nearly 9 million. But much of the city was devastated and thousands were killed during the Blitz in World War II. By the 1960s, postwar austerity had given way to 'swinging London', a leader in fashion, music and pop culture. The regeneration of the Docklands, new architecture, ambitious millennium projects and preparations for the Olympic Games in 2012 have given London an optimistic outlook for the 21st century.

⬤ *The Cenotaph in Whitehall – a memorial for those killed during two world wars*

Lifestyle

London is always on the go. As the country's major transportation hub – with five airports, eleven mainline rail stations, and dozens more Tube and rail stops – there are thousands of travellers coming and going every day. The pace of life is quick and busy in the city, and why not? London has a lot to offer, and between working, commuting, socialising, shopping and a bit of culture, there's a lot to pack in. If you want to see Londoners relax, head for a pub. Every neighbourhood has its 'local', where friends catch up and shake off the day's cares over a pint.

London is a cosmopolitan city. Its residents come from all over the world and all walks of life. Many come to study or for work or business opportunities, and end up staying much longer than intended. London's rainbow population has made it a tolerant city, where cultures and ideas can be freely expressed. This freestyle attitude has brought London much admiration in the art and fashion worlds.

As a centre of business and finance, London is largely a prosperous city. Visitors may find London expensive, especially if the exchange rate isn't in their favour, but in reality the cost of hotels and restaurants is no worse than in most other cities of its size and stature. For Londoners, to have such a wealth of culture, entertainment and services at their fingertips, it's worth it.

Amid the hustle and bustle of the city, Hyde Park offers a gentler way to be

Culture

London is one of the world's great cities for art and culture. It is the repository of the nation's finest treasures, collected not just in Britain but from around the world. Three outstanding galleries form the backbone of London's art world: the National Gallery houses a magnificent collection of Western European art; Tate Modern is one of the largest and most highly-rated modern art museums in the world; and Tate Britain is dedicated to British art spanning more than five centuries.

London is a perfect city to explore culture in the broader sense. The British Museum holds a record of mankind from prehistoric times to the present day. The extensive range of decorative arts at the Victoria and Albert Museum is a window into everyday culture over the centuries.

Modern culture in all its forms is also given a showcase in London. The Design Museum presents everyday objects from the 20th and 21st centuries as art forms. The London Transport Museum, Theatre Museum and Science Museum all show different facets of British culture and lifestyle.

Of course, culture often means the performing arts, and there is no shortage of them in London. It has one of the most renowned theatre scenes in the world, with more than 50 West End theatres (and many more in the greater metropolitan area) offering productions ranging from Shakespeare and the classics to works by cutting-edge playwrights. Traditional opera is staged at the Royal Opera House, and English-language opera productions at the Coliseum. Both venues also stage ballet. But for dance, the Sadler's

The Aldwych Theatre opened in 1905

⬢ *Some musicals have been running for years*

Wells Theatre is one of the finest venues in Europe. London also has many fine venues for classical music, from large concert halls such as the Royal Albert Hall to intimate stages like the Purcell Room at the South Bank Centre. Whatever your tastes, London offers rich pickings for culture vultures.

▶ *St Paul's Cathedral dominates the City*

Shopping

London ranks alongside Paris and New York as one of the best shopping cities in the world. Affluent residents and visitors have kept upmarket shops such as Asprey, the royal jeweller, and the bespoke tailors of Savile Row in business for centuries. But there is a shopping scene to suit every budget, from designer labels to funky fashions to middle of the road department stores that offer something for everybody.

Sadly, the big high-street chains have squeezed out many of the more interesting, one-off shops in many parts of London, but you can still find pockets with unique offerings. One of these is Covent Garden's Neal Street, which caters to a hip, alternative crowd. Markets, particularly Camden Town and Spitalfields, are a good place to look for cutting edge street and club wear, often by young, up-and-coming designers.

Oxford Street, between Oxford Circus and Marble Arch, has several good department stores and large branches of major chains such as Gap and Marks and Spencer. Consequently, it's probably the most crowded shopping street in the capital. Head off into the side streets either side of Bond Street tube for more interesting, if pricier shopping, where you'll find fashion shops such as Whistles in St Christopher's Place. Bond Street itself is a byword for exclusive shopping, whether it be jewellery at Tiffany, leather goods at Mulberry, or men's and women's designer clothing. Knightsbridge is another area for upmarket fashion, particularly in the triangle between Brompton Road, Sloane Street and Sloane Avenue, where you'll find Harrods and Harvey Nichols as well as Joseph, Kenzo and Jimmy Choo. These days, Chelsea's famous King's Road is a mixed bag of shops selling trendy shoes and clothing, and goods that appeal to well-heeled young families.

Borough Market (Fri–Sat) is one of the best places to indulge your food fantasies, but there are good Italian delis and specialist food shops in Soho and many other parts of the city. The food halls at Harrods and Fortnum and Mason are great places for foodie gifts and treats. Home furnishings are another hot shopping topic, with many good speciality shops in Chelsea and along Tottenham Court Road near Goodge Street station.

🔺 *The most famous department store in London*

Eating & drinking

London has a huge range of restaurants and cafés catering to all tastes and budgets. One of the great joys of eating out here is the diversity of the ethnic restaurants, reflecting the mix of cultures in the capital. Londoners' insatiable interest in discovering new foods and tastes ensures that there are plenty of food shops, markets and department-store grocery sections across the city to provide for an impromptu picnic in the park.

⬤ *Eating al fresco while the sun shines*

Eating

Many restaurants open for lunch around 12.00 and serve until 14.30 or 15.00, then reopen for dinner around 18.00 until 23.30. Depending on the menu, many will also stay open all day. Most have slightly longer hours at the weekend. Many cafés serve breakfast from around 08.00, earlier in residential neighbourhoods. Some restaurants close on Sunday or Monday, but most are open seven days a week.

If you want to try the cuisine at an expensive restaurant but are worried about the cost, consider going there at lunchtime. Many have two- or three-course set menus at lunchtime (some at dinnertime, too) that are very good value. Some pre-theatre menus can offer good value, although the choice will be restricted. If you're watching the budget, pub meals are one of the cheapest options and can be very satisfying. Most restaurants have vegetarian dishes on the menu, and there are dedicated vegetarian restaurants around town as well.

It's a good idea, and often essential, to book ahead for any restaurant that is popular or currently fashionable. A service charge of 10–12 per cent (more for large parties) is often included in the bill. If not, a tip of that amount is customary, and you may want to leave a bit more on top for good service.

Drinking

The wine is as important as the food in many restaurants, and you will generally find a good range of new- and old-world wines on the

---

RESTAURANT CATEGORIES
£ = up to £15   ££ = £15–30   £££ = above £30
(average price of a three-course meal without drinks)

menu, often with several available by the glass. Cocktail bars are back in fashion, and there are plenty of wine bars around the city. Beer lovers looking for the best choice and opportunity to try a new and unusual brew should look for pubs and bars that serve real ales. There are several in the City and around Borough Market.

Hundreds of coffee bars have sprung up around the capital and an assortment of black and flavoured tea is also now widely available.

Do it yourself

With its many parks and squares, London is a prime spot for picnicking on a fine day. The green expanses of Hyde Park or St James's Park are good city-centre options, but don't neglect the smaller patches such as Soho Square or Russell Square, which offer convenient breaks from sightseeing. There are many options for do-it-yourself dining, from take-away sushi to salads. Sandwich bars and chains such as Pret-a-Manger have a great choice of breads and fillings. Markets, delis and specialist food shops are another good source, selling cheeses, olives and other picnic supplies.

Local specialities

Old British favourites such as steak and kidney pudding, sausages, roast beef and even fish and chips are given the star treatment at gastropubs and in kitchens run by enthusiastic young chefs reinventing their culinary roots. For real London fare, look for a traditional pie and mash shop serving savoury pies, mashed potatoes and fresh eels; there are still a few in the East End.

● *'London overspill' at the most popular pubs and bars during summer*

Entertainment & nightlife

There is no end of options for enjoying London's thriving nightlife. No matter what kind of entertainment you desire, it is probably happening somewhere in the capital.

London is famous round the world for its high-quality theatre, and most visitors want to take in a production or two. More than 50 theatres make up London's West End Theatre District, and there are highly rated off-West End venues that are well worth seeking out. In the summer there are open-air productions in Regent's Park and Holland Park. A good source of information is the Society of London Theatre's website 🆆 www.officiallondontheatre.co.uk.

You can book tickets at the theatre itself, or through a ticket agency such as Ticketmaster (☎ 0870 534 4444 🆆 www.ticketmaster.co.uk) or First Call (☎ 0870 906 3700 🆆 www.firstcalltickets.com) but beware of high surcharges charged by the agencies. The TKTS booth in Leicester Square sells half-price tickets for same-day performances for many theatres, though the most popular shows are rarely among them. Avoid ticket touts – their prices are high and their tickets may be bogus.

Fans of classical music, dance and opera will also find a rich banquet from which to choose. The main venues include the Royal Albert Hall and Royal Festival Hall for concerts, Sadler's Wells Theatre for dance, and the Royal Opera House and the Coliseum for opera and ballet. There are many smaller venues with cultural entertainment around the city, and outdoor concerts in Hyde Park and Hampstead Heath in summer. Buy tickets through the venue or listings agencies.

London is heaven for cinema-goers, from the diversity of films at the National Film Theatre to the blockbusters that premiere at the state-of-the-art Empire and Odeon cinemas in Leicester Square. London's best cinemas include the Screen on the Green in Islington, the Gate in Notting Hill and the Renoir near Russell Square, for their character as well as their art-house and foreign language showings.

The West End is teeming with hugely successful musicals

Around 150 new international films are screened at the London Film Festival in late October/early November.

The city's music and nightlife scene is exciting. You can drink in music bars, comedy clubs, characterful pubs or smart cocktail bars with great views over the skyline. On any given night you can hear live jazz, rock, roots and dance music in a variety of venues, from tiny basement clubs to pubs to concert halls. An increasing number of DJ bars also fill the gap between pub and club. London's big nightclubs are world famous, attracting top DJs from around the world. Some of the best are located on the fringes of the city centre. At weekends you can dance all night till long after dawn, but clubbing goes on every night of the week, with theme nights and dance music of all styles. There are also many gay bars and clubs.

Listings media

The most comprehensive source of listings for live music, clubs and concerts is *Time Out* magazine, which is published weekly. It has good reviews of artists, bands and venues and also has listings for film, theatre, dance, art exhibitions and other events around town. The major newspapers all have listings for theatre and cultural events in their entertainment pages, with more in-depth guides to what's on and reviews in their Saturday and Sunday supplements. The London *Evening Standard* is focussed on the capital, with comprehensive listings in their Thursday magazine.

▶ *The Royal Opera House is one of London's most prestigious venues*

Sport & relaxation

As the host city for the 2012 Olympics, London's sports stature has never been higher. Top sporting venues like Wembly and Wimbledon will be joined by new purpose-built arenas in East London's Olympic Park, including a stadium, aquatics centre and a velodrome. Football is the most popular sport in the capital, with two of England's top clubs, Arsenal and Chelsea, based here. There are also top tennis courts, cricket pitches and rugby grounds, and horse-racing nearby at Epsom Downs, Kempton Park and Sandown Park. London's parks provide great opportunities for participant sports.

SPECTATOR SPORTS

The following are some of London's most famous sporting venues. You can get tickets to sporting events from the venues or from ticket agencies (see page 28).

Cricket London is home base for two county teams. Middlesex play at **Lord's** Cricket Ground ⓐ St John's Wood NW8 ⓣ 020 7432 1000 ⓦ www.lords.org.uk ⓝ St John's Wood. Surrey play at the **Oval** ⓐ Kennington SE11 ⓣ 020 7582 6660 ⓦ www.surreycricket.com

⬤ *Spectating can be as entertaining as participating*

Oval. Both grounds host test matches, one-day internationals and Twenty20 Cup matches.

Football (soccer) matches are highly popular, especially those for teams in the Barclays Premiership league. **Arsenal Football Club** is at Emirates Stadium, Ashburton Grove N7 020 7704 4040 www.arsenal.com Arsenal. **Chelsea Football Club** is at Stamford Bridge, Fulham Road SW6 0870 300 1212 www.chelseafc.co.uk Fulham Broadway
For information on all London clubs, visit www.thefa.com

Tennis The world's oldest tennis championship is held each summer at the famous All England Lawn Tennis Club in Wimbledon 020 8946 2244 www.wimbledon.org Southfields

PARTICIPANT SPORTS

Cycling, **Jogging**, **Walking** Hyde Park and Kensington Gardens provide the largest expanse in central London for these activities. Hampstead Heath is also a prime spot. Skate rental is available at **Slick Willies** 41 Kensington High Street 020 7937 3824 High Street Kensington

Golf There are a number of golf clubs in outer London and you don't have to be a member to play. For a list of courses contact the English Golf Union 01526 354500 www.englishgolfunion.org

Swimming There are pools at **Oasis Sports Centre** 32 Endell Street, Covent Garden 020 7831 1804 www.camden.gov.uk and **Central YMCA** 112 Great Russell Street 020 7343 1700 www.centralYMCA.org.uk

Accommodation

It's not cheap to stay in London. Accommodation is generally more expensive in all price categories than its counterpart in most other European cities. Accommodation ranges from bed-and-breakfast establishments, apartment hotels, small private hotels and townhouse hotels, to international chains. There are also youth hostels for budget travellers.

An important factor to consider when choosing a hotel in central London is noise. If you're a light sleeper, look for hotels on quieter

⬤ *Many of London's hotels are housed in magnificent buildings*

side streets or residential areas. Hotel prices generally include VAT (tax) but not always breakfast, so when booking be sure to ask what services and facilities are included in the quoted price.

You can find some charming B&Bs that are welcoming and full of character, but many at the cheaper end, such as those around Earl's Court, can be very basic, so choose with care. **Uptown Reservations** ➋ 8 Kelso Place, Kensington W8 5QD ➊ 020 7937 2001 ⓦ www.uptownres.co.uk has a list of elegant B&Bs in host homes full of antiques and architectural interest.

When choosing an area, keep in mind that the more central you are, the more you're likely to pay. Upmarket areas like Covent Garden and Soho, Kensington and Chelsea, and Notting Hill will cost more than areas on their fringes, such as Bloomsbury, Earl's Court, or Paddington and Bayswater, which are just as convenient for sightseeing. Don't dismiss outlying areas, especially if they are near a Tube line or good bus route, though you may want to ask advice from the tourist board or a knowledgeable friend as to their suitability.

It's not easy to find a bargain in London. To get the best prices and the most desirable hotels, you must book well in advance. You will find the best deals by booking over the internet, either via the hotel's own website or through websites that specialise in

PRICE RATING

Hotels in England are rated from one to five 'crowns' based on the facilities they offer, while the classifications 'approved', 'commended', 'highly commended' and 'deluxe' give an indication of quality. The ratings in this book are as follows:
£ = up to £85 **££** = £85–£150 **£££** = over £150
All prices are for a single night in a double room/two persons.

accommodation and travel. You are also likely to save money by booking a combination flight-hotel package.
A few websites to try include:

ⓦ www.londontown.com
ⓦ www.expedia.co.uk or ⓦ www.expedia.com
ⓦ www.lastminute.com
ⓦ www.priceline.co.uk
ⓦ www.hotelpronto.com
ⓦ www.activehotels.co.uk

Visit London (see page 152) publishes *Where to Stay in London*, a guide to inspected properties in all accommodation categories. It lists prices and facilities, and is available from tourist information centres and bookshops. Visit London has an accommodation hotline where you can book by phone with a credit card (ⓣ 0845 644 3010 ⓛ 0900–1800). London tourist offices (see pages 152–153) also have a room-booking service for a small fee. The **British Hotel Reservation Centre** (ⓦ www.bhrc.co.uk) has desks at Heathrow, Gatwick and Victoria rail and coach stations ⓛ 0600–2400.

HOSTELS

City of London Hostel £ This large YHA hostel with a great location across from St Paul's Cathedral has dorm rooms sleeping up to eight people, a few twin rooms and a café. ⓐ 36 Carter Lane ⓣ 020 7236 4965 ⓔ city@yha.org.uk ⓝ St Paul's

Piccadilly Backpackers Hostel £ Sleep in Japanese-style pods, arranged in uniquely decorated domitory rooms, off Piccadilly Circus

---

▶ *Set back from the Strand, the Savoy exudes luxury*

and handy for Heathrow airport. ⓐ 12 Sherwood Street ⓣ 020 7434 9009 ⓦ www.piccadillyhotel.net ⓝ Piccadilly Circus

HOTELS & B&BS

B&B Belgravia ££ Stylish B&B with big sash windows, mosaic tiled bathrooms and modern furnishings, a short walk from Victoria coach and rail stations. ⓐ 64–66 Ebury Street ⓣ 020 7823 4928 ⓦ www.bb-belgravia.com ⓝ Victoria

The Gainsborough ££ Beautifully furnished rooms in a Georgian townhouse, in a quiet location near the Natural History Museum. ⓐ 7–11 Queensberry Place ⓣ 020 7957 0000 ⓦ www.hotelgainsborough.co.uk ⓝ South Kensington

St Margaret's Hotel ££ At just under £100 including breakfast, this simple hotel is a good budget option and is well located in Bloomsbury near the British Museum. ⓐ 26 Bedford Place ⓣ 020 7636 4277 ⓦ www.stmargaretshotel.co.uk ⓝ Russell Square

Claridge's £££ A London landmark, with large, luxurious rooms, elegant decor and impeccable service, a stone's throw from the shops on Bond Street. ⓐ Brook Street ⓣ 020 7629 8860 ⓦ www.claridgeshotel.com ⓝ Bond Street

Miller's Residence £££ Stuffed with antiques and brimming with ambience, this grand B&B looks like a movie set and is located in a trendy Notting Hill neighbourhood. ⓐ 111a Westbourne Grove ⓣ 020 7243 1024 ⓦ www.millersuk.com ⓝ Bayswater

---

▶ *Tea – or more – at the Ritz is a great treat for a special occasion*

THE BEST OF LONDON

London has so much to offer, you could spend a year here and still not see it all. There is something to interest everyone, so even if you only have a day or two, London is a great place for a fun-filled weekend break. If you're visiting on business or for a trade fair, there's plenty to do after hours, too. In addition to nightlife and theatre, shops and many museums have late-night opening one or two days a week.

TOP 10 ATTRACTIONS

- **Tower of London** Centuries of history and the Crown Jewels lie within the massive walls of this London landmark (see page 107).

- **London Eye** Relax and be thrilled as the glass pod carries you to the top for stunning panoramas of the city (see page 118).

- **Covent Garden** The old covered market is now one of London's liveliest spots for shopping, dining and entertainment (see page 62).

- **British Museum** Remarkable treasures from ancient times and from around the world fill the galleries of this venerable museum (see page 66).

- **St Paul's Cathedral** Its landmark dome is the second-largest in the world (see page 106).

- **Tate Modern** London's impressive modern art gallery is set in the former Bankside Power Station on the banks of the Thames (see page 122).

- **Big Ben** A symbol of London around the world, the beloved clock tower adjoins the House of Parliament (see page 80).

- **Boat cruise on the Thames** Discover London's landmarks on an entertaining riverboat cruise (see page 82).

- **Westminster Abbey** The crowning place of monarchs through the ages, it has some of London's finest medieval architecture (see page 82).

- **National Gallery** A superb collection of great art that spans eight centuries (see page 66).

Buckingham Palace attracts thousands of visitors each year

Your at-a-glance guide to seeing the best that London has to offer, depending on how much time you have.

HALF-DAY: LONDON IN A HURRY

Stick to the central area to see several London highlights in a short time. Begin at Covent Garden with its lively scene around the historic covered market. Then stroll through the back streets lined with interesting shops to Trafalgar Square, which is only a few minutes away. Spend an hour or so seeing the highlights in the National Gallery. You could also pop in to St Martin-in-the-Fields church or the National Portrait Gallery. Then wander down to the Victoria Embankment for some fine riverside views, and carry on to Westminster for a close-up look at Big Ben, the Houses of Parliament and Westminster Abbey. Return to Covent Garden or Soho for a wider choice of cafés and restaurants.

1 DAY: TIME TO SEE A LITTLE MORE

With the other half of the day to spare, walk across Westminster Bridge to the London Eye for the most fantastic views over the city. If you've booked a time slot ahead, you won't have to waste time queuing. From here it's about a half-hour walk along the river promenade to the Tate Modern; if you're tired, take the Tube from Waterloo to London Bridge. Have a snack at the gallery's café and take in some of the collection. Then walk across the Millennium Bridge to St Paul's Cathedral. Take the Tube to Holborn and stroll through the streets of Covent Garden back to the piazza.

2–3 DAYS: SHORT CITY BREAK

With a couple more days you can get a much broader impression of the city and take in some of its bigger attractions as well as those mentioned above. Both the Tower of London and the British Museum are highlights, but will require at least two hours (or more) each to do them justice. A boat cruise on the River Thames is fun and can get you to or from the Tower. A stroll in Hyde Park or Kensington Gardens makes a refreshing change from urban sightseeing. You should also explore London's great nightlife, whether you take in a musical or drama at a West End theatre or dance the night away at a trendy nightclub.

LONGER: ENJOYING LONDON TO THE FULL

At least a week is needed to get beyond the surface attractions and begin to get a feel for the real London. Once you've hit the main sights, fan out to some of the areas around the city centre, where you'll discover the breadth and depth of London's architecture, history and multicultural lifestyle. Spend some time exploring the streets of the East End, Southwark, Chelsea or Hampstead, enjoying their markets, pubs and cafés. A day-trip to Hampton Court Palace or Greenwich is also recommended.

● *Cart yourself around Covent Garden's cobbles by historic stagecoach*

Something for nothing

London may be an expensive city, but there are plenty of ways to enjoy yourself while spending very little, or, in many cases, nothing at all.

Britain's capital has some of the finest museums in the world, and best of all, they're free. You can ogle antiquities in the British Museum, drool over the decorative arts at the V&A, admire the great masters at the National Gallery and National Portrait Gallery, all without spending a penny. Other top museums where admission is free include the Tate Britain and the Tate Modern, the Natural History Museum, the Science Museum, the Imperial War Museum, the National Maritime Museum and the Museum of London. You might have to pay for any special exhibitions, but there is free entry to the main collections. Other museums and galleries may have free or reduced admission one day or evening a month.

Although St Paul's Cathedral and Westminster Abbey have hefty admission charges, there are many smaller churches around the city with lovely architecture and interiors that cost nothing to see. There's an ongoing free show from the street performers at Covent Garden piazza (but do be generous when they pass the hat). Churches all over London have free lunchtime concerts throughout the year (donations appreciated), ranging from organ recitals to chamber music to solos performed by professional musicians. St Martin-in-the-Fields (Trafalgar Square), St Bride's (Fleet Street) and St Mary-le-Bow (Cheapside) are some of the well-known venues. The Royal Academy of Music (Marylebone) and the Royal College of Music (South Kensington) also presents free lunchtime concerts during term time.

Browsing in London's street markets costs nothing, and it's a great way to pick up the flavour of the city. The capital's wonderful green spaces – Hyde Park, St James's Park, Regent's Park and Hampstead Heath, to name a few – are also part of the London experience and can be freely enjoyed by all.

While children under 11 can ride London's buses and the Tube for free, the only free transport for adults is on foot. But you'll see more that way and keep fit, too. Walking along the South Bank, Piccadilly or across a London bridge, you'll feel very rich indeed.

● *A green pocket of serenity in the middle of Leicester Square*

When it rains

Rain is a frequent fact of life in London, but it needn't spoil your holiday fun. A rainy day is the obvious time to visit one of London's big museums, and you may allow yourself a more in-depth visit than if the sunshine was beckoning outside.

If you have children, entertain them at the Science Museum or the Natural History Museum. A rainy day is also a good time to visit St Martin-in-the-Fields church, which has a brass-rubbing centre in the crypt. If you need to burn off excess energy, there are two good sports centres in the city centre. The Central YMCA on Great Russell Street has day memberships that allow the use of the pool, gym and other facilities. At the Oasis Sports Centre in Covent Garden, fees to use the pools, sauna, gym and other facilities are inexpensive.

Shopping is another good way to spend a rainy day. Many of London's big department stores are clustered together along Oxford Street, so you won't get very wet dashing between them.

When all else fails, simply linger over coffee and cakes at a popular café or patisserie, or park yourself in an atmospheric pub. There's no better place for people-watching on a rainy day.

▶ *While away the hours in the British Museum*

On arrival

Travellers arriving by plane will land at one of five airports serving London. All have good public transport connections into the city centre.

TIME DIFFERENCES

London is in the Greenwich Mean Time (GMT) zone, from which time is measured around the globe. Clocks are put forward by one hour during British Summer Time, end March–end Oct. Time differences from GMT are:

Australia +8 hours (west coast) to +11 hours (east coast)

Canada –3¹/₂ hours (Newfoundland) to –5 hours (east coast) to –8 hours (west coast)

New Zealand +13 hours

South Africa +2 hours

USA –5 hours (east coast) to –8 hours (west coast)

Western Europe + 1 hour to +2 hours

ARRIVING

By air

Heathrow Airport ☎ 0870 000 0123 🌐 www.baa.co.uk/heathrow is about 19 km (12 miles) west of central London.

The London Underground (Tube) Piccadilly line connects the airport to the city centre. The journey takes about an hour and currently costs £4. Trains run from approximately 05.30–23.45 daily. Buy tickets in the ticket hall before boarding the train. Heathrow Express trains run directly to Paddington station from the airport Tube stations and takes about 15–20 minutes. They run every 15 minutes from 05.10–00.08. Tickets cost £14 single and £26 return;

discounts are available when booked in advance ☎ 0845 600 1515
🌐 www.heathrowexpress.co.uk

National Express coaches run to London Victoria station, leaving approximately every 30 minutes between 05.35 and 21.35. The journey takes around 90 minutes, depending on traffic, and costs £10 single, £15 return. ☎ 08705 808080 🌐 www.nationalexpress.com

There are taxi ranks outside the terminals and the one-hour journey to the city centre costs from £50–£100.

Gatwick Airport ☎ 0870 000 2468 🌐 www.baa.co.uk/gatwick is about 50 km (30 miles) south of central London.

Various train lines connect the city to the airport, but the fastest and easiest is the Gatwick Express from Victoria Station (☎ 0845 850 1530 🌐 www.gatwickexpress.co.uk). It runs at 03.30, 04.30, then every 15 minutes from 05.00–23.45, last train at 00.30. The journey takes 30 minutes and costs £13 single, £24 return (valid for 30 days). A taxi will cost around £80–£100 and will take between 1 and 2 hours, depending on traffic.

London City Airport ☎ 020 7646 0000 🌐 www.londoncityairport. com lies to the east of the city centre, about 14 km (9 miles). It is heavily used by business travellers, and has meeting rooms and business facilities.

The airport is a designated stop on the Docklands Light Railway. Trains run from 05.30–00.30 weekdays and 07.00–23.30 weekends; it takes about 20 minutes into the city centre. The Blue Shuttlebus leaves every 15 minutes from 06.30–21.30. The ride to Liverpool Street station takes 25 minutes via Canary Wharf and costs £6.50; pay the driver (cash) when you board. A taxi to central London costs around £20–£30.

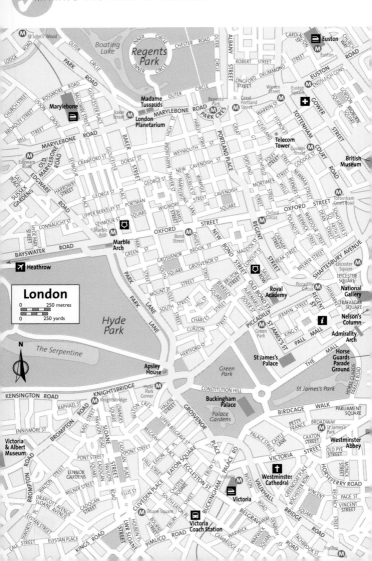

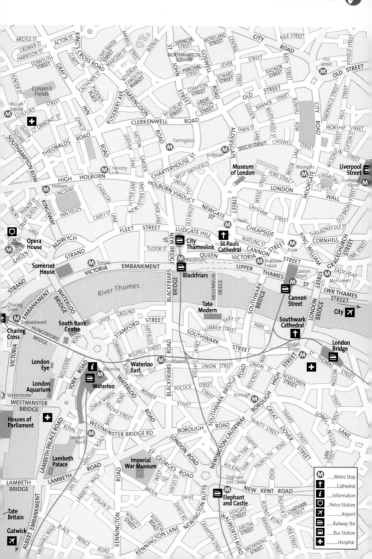

Luton Airport ☎ 01582 405100 ⓦ www.london-luton.com is about 50 km (30 miles) north of London and is used by several budget airlines. There is a Thameslink rail service from King's Cross to Luton Airport Parkway Station, and then a shuttle bus to the airport. Trains run approximately every 30 minutes and the journey takes 35–45 minutes. Fares are £10.70 single, £19.70 return.

Greenline (☎ 0870 608 7261 ⓦ www.greenline.co.uk) operates around-the-clock coach service between the airport and convenient locations in central London, leaving every 20–30 minutes at peak times. Fares are £10.50 single, £15 return and the trip takes 60–90 minutes. Taxis take between 1½ and 2 hours and cost from £50.

Stansted Airport ☎ 0870 0000 0303 ⓦ www.stanstedairport.com is about 56 km (35 miles) northeast of London in Essex. The Stansted Express rail service (☎ 0845 748 4950 ⓦ www.stanstedexpress.com) runs to and from London's Liverpool Street station, every 15–45 minutes. It operates from 04.30 or 04.55 to 22.55 or 23.25. The journey takes 40–45 minutes and costs £15 single, £25 return.

There is 24-hour coach service to and from Victoria Station on the Airbus (☎ 0870 580 8080 ⓦ www.nationalexpress.com). Coaches leave every 30 minutes and the journey takes 1½ hours or more; fares are £10 single, £15 return. A taxi from Stansted costs around £80 and takes 1–2 hours.

By rail

Eurostar trains from France and Belgium arrive at London's Waterloo station, where passengers must clear passport control and customs. The London Underground (Tube), buses, taxis and suburban trains link the station with the rest of the capital.

Trains also link the ferry ports to central London. Passengers from ports on the south coast will arrive at Victoria, passengers from Harwich will arrive at Liverpool Street. For national rail, trains from various parts of the country arrive at London's 11 main rail stations: Charing Cross, Euston, Fenchurch Street, King's Cross, Liverpool Street, London Bridge, Marylebone, Paddington, St Pancras, Victoria and Waterloo. All have bus, taxi, tube and rail links for onward journeys, and most parts of the capital can be reached in 30–60 minutes or less. There are tourist offices at Victoria, Liverpool Street and Waterloo.

Waterloo International Terminal ❶ 0870 518 6186
Ⓦ www.eurostar.com
National Rail Enquiries ❶ 0845 748 4950 Ⓦ www.nationalrail.co.uk

By coach

Long-distance coaches, whether domestic or from the Continent, arrive at Victoria Coach Station. The Victoria tube and rail station is a short walk away, and there are city buses and taxi ranks as well.

Eurolines ❶ 01582 404511 Ⓦ www.eurolines.com operates coach services to Europe.
National Express is the main carrier for domestic routes.
❶ 0870 580 8080 Ⓦ www.nationalexpress.com

By road

If you drive, be aware of the exorbitant Congestion Charge (£8) that is charged daily for taking your car into the eight square miles of central London between 07.00 and 18.30 Mon–Fri. Even if your car is simply parked within the zone and not driven, the charge applies.

© Transport for London

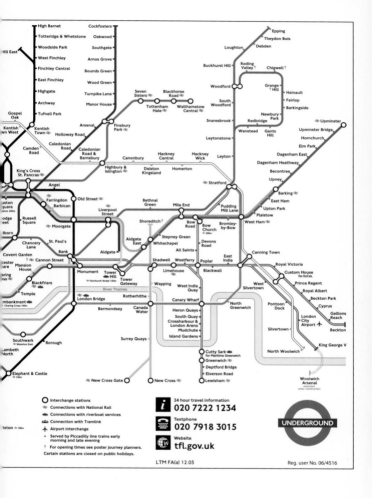

Road signs and red 'C's painted on the road indicate that you are entering the zone. You can pay by credit card over the phone ❶ 0845 900 1234 or online ❿ www.cclondon.com; passes can also be purchased at newsagents, garages and NCP car parks. You can pay in advance or any time on the day you enter the zone, but do so before 22.00 or there will be a £2 surcharge. If you fail to pay by midnight, you will be fined £100.

FINDING YOUR FEET

Although London is a big city, most of the main tourist attractions are centrally located. It is easy and indeed most enjoyable to walk between them. In compact areas such as Covent Garden, Soho and Piccadilly, it is often quicker to walk than to take public transport. There are some seedy areas around King's Cross and other outlying regions, but the central tourist areas are generally safe, even at night. Perhaps the biggest danger for visitors from some countries is remembering that traffic drives on the left-hand side, so look both ways before crossing the street.

ORIENTATION

The River Thames winds through central London, dividing the city into north and south. Most of the areas of interest to visitors lie within a mile or two inland from its banks. Landmarks such as St Paul's Cathedral and the Tower of London in the east, and Big Ben or Marble Arch in the west, can help you to get your bearings.

On the north side of the river, the main thoroughfare running east to west from the City to West London is Holborn-Oxford Street-Bayswater Road. Several bridges cross the Thames and there are two

❿ *Black cab drivers have the 'knowledge' to take you wherever you need to go*

pedestrian bridges: the Hungerford Bridge from Embankment to the South Bank, and the new Millennium Bridge, linking St Paul's Cathedral and Tate Modern. Two ornate Victorian bridges are landmarks at either end of the city centre: Tower Bridge in the east and Albert Bridge in Chelsea.

The maps in this book and those from the tourist office show the main sights and streets, but London is filled with smaller streets and passages. If you plan to be in London for any length of time, pick up a copy of the London Streetfinder, better known as the A-Z, which is the visitor's bible for navigating the city.

GETTING AROUND

London has an extensive public transport system of underground and overland trains, buses and the Docklands Light Railway (DLR). Generally, the fastest way to get to most tourist areas and attractions is to use the London Underground, known as the Tube. However, delays are common and it is very hot and crowded, especially during rush hours (08.00–09.30 and 16.30–19.00 weekdays). Several lines criss-cross the city, denoted by different

◯ The computerised DLR trains take you from the city out east and south

colours on the Tube map. Many stations serve two or more lines, making interchanges easy and fairly frequent, though you may have to walk a long way between platforms.

The Tube network is divided into six zones and priced accordingly. Single fares are expensive, starting at £3 for a single journey in zones 1–4. It is much more cost effective to buy a Travelcard. There are a number of options. There are one- and three-day Travelcards, which can cover from two to six zones. Off-peak Travelcards (after 09.30 weekdays and all day weekends) are cheaper than those that allow rush-hour travel, and start at £4.90 for two zones. Travelcards can also be used on buses and the DLR. Children aged 11 and under can travel free when accompanied by an adult.

The cheapest way to travel is to buy an Oyster card, which can be used on the Tube, buses and some overland trains. It can be used as a seven-day, monthly or longer Travelcard, or you can opt to put up to £90 on the card and pay as you go. Single fares using Oyster cards start at £1.50. If you make a number of journeys in one day, you will never be charged more than the price of a day Travelcard.

For more information, see the London Regional Transport website ⓦ www.tfl.gov.uk. You can get Oyster cards online at ⓦ www.sales.oystercard.com or by calling ☎ 0845 330 9876. You can buy them along with travel cards at Tube stations, newsagents and London travel information centres.

London's famous red Routemaster buses have been phased out in favour of new 'bendy-buses' with low floors, which are more accessible to pushchairs and wheelchairs. For many buses in central London you must now buy a ticket before you board, from a pavement ticket machine. Travelcards and Oyster cards can be used on buses, and there are one-day bus passes as well. Single fares are £1.50 (80p or £1 with an Oyster card). Children under 16 travel free, but 14- and 15-year-olds need a photocard. Books of six Saver tickets can be purchased at newsagents.

Bus routes and timetables are posted at the bus stops. Services run every 10–30 minutes, depending on the route and on traffic. Night buses have the prefix 'N'; many leave from Trafalgar Square. Buses may not stop automatically at all stops, especially in outlying areas; when the bus number you want is approaching, flag it down.

You can pick up Tube and bus maps at tourist information centres as well as many Tube stations.

London's licensed taxis, known as 'black cabs', now come in a variety of colours. If the 'For Hire' sign on top is lit, it can be hailed on the street. Or look for a taxi rank at major railway stations and hotels. Black cabs are metered and higher rates apply at night and on weekends. Minicabs are usually cheaper than black cabs, and are sometimes the best alternative outside the centre, where finding black cabs can be hit and miss. Make sure you use a licensed minicab, designated by a yellow disc. Avoid those who tout for business on the street, as they may be unlicensed and uninsured. Always ask and agree the price to your destination in advance when booking, and confirm it with the driver when they arrive. Minicab firms are listed in the telephone directory.

CAR HIRE

Car hire is not recommended in London, due to the difficulty and cost of parking, and the congestion charge. It is much quicker and easier to get around by public transport. If you must, all the major car hire firms are represented at the airports. The tourist information office can advise on local firms.

▶ *The 'mother of parliaments', Westminster Palace*

THE CITY

Central London 1

SOHO, COVENT GARDEN & BLOOMSBURY

Metre for metre, this area of central London is the most pulsating part of the city. Between Charing Cross rail station in the south and King's Cross station in the north lie some of its best-known names and faces: the bustling, modern-day market at Covent Garden, the thriving nightlife of Soho, the literary delights of Bloomsbury and historic Holborn. Here you'll find some of London's most important museums, trendiest shopping and no end of good restaurants, bars and pubs.

The compact streets around Covent Garden, Leicester Square and Soho are best seen on foot and indeed walking is often the quickest way between them. The area is also well served by numerous Tube stations.

SIGHTS & ATTRACTIONS

Covent Garden

When the former fruit and vegetable market here moved to the suburbs in the 1970s, the Victorian market halls and surrounding piazza were transformed into London's liveliest square. Now speciality shops and jewellery, clothes and craft stalls trade beneath the iron-roofed arcades, while the wide cobbled square between the market and St Paul's church is an open-air stage for energetic street performers who always draw a crowd. The surrounding streets are home to delightful specialist shops, making Covent Garden a favourite with Londoners who meet here for a spot of shopping before going off to the many theatres, pubs and wine bars. Ⓝ Covent Garden

Leicester Square

Leicester Square's main attraction is its location, a meeting point midway between Covent Garden and Soho and one of the few green patches in this part of the city. It's crowded at lunchtimes, but if you're lucky you might find a spot to perch with your sandwich. At night, the square is teeming with nightlife and people heading for the surrounding cinemas and nearby nightclubs and theatres. On the south side of the square is a TKTS booth selling half-price theatre tickets for same-day performances.

Ⓦ www.officiallondontheatre.co.uk for half-price tickets
Ⓛ Booth open 10.00–19.00 Mon–Sat, 12.00–15.30 Sun for matinees
Ⓝ Leicester Square

Piccadilly Circus

Despite its whimsical name, this London landmark is little more than a massive roundabout teeming with traffic at the junction of five major West End streets. Nonetheless, the giant neon billboards that have been flashing here for nearly a century give it a certain urban excitement. Ⓝ Piccadilly Circus

St Martin-in-the-Fields

This graceful church on the north-eastern side of Trafalgar Square was designed by architect James Gibbs in the 1720s to look like a classical temple. There are free lunchtime concerts of classical music several days a week, and a brass-rubbing centre in the crypt. The church is also admired for its work with London's homeless.

Ⓐ Trafalgar Square Ⓣ 020 7766 1100 Ⓦ www.stmartin-in-the-fields.org Ⓛ 08.00–18.30 Mon–Sat, 08.00–19.30 Sun Ⓝ Leicester Square, Charing Cross

Soho & Chinatown

A byword for all that is hip and happening in the capital, Soho is by day the centre of the film, advertising and media industries, by night a mecca for clubbers and bar-hoppers out on the town. In the 1960s and 1970s Soho was associated with sleaze and a few porn shops remain, but even these can't tarnish its ascent as the shiniest star in London's night sky. Cinemas, clubs, restaurants and theatres crowd the streets. Ⓝ Leicester Square

Trafalgar Square

London's great square is the focal point for all kinds of mass gatherings, from political demonstrations to New Year's Eve celebrations to flocks of tourists and pigeons who come to perch on its fountains and monuments, the tallest of which is Nelson's Column, at 56 m (184 ft) to commemorate the admiral's final naval victory. Notice the controversial statue by Alison Lapper. The square is the departure point for London's night buses.
Ⓝ Charing Cross, Leicester Square

CULTURE

British Library

If you've got some time to kill at King's Cross station, it's worth taking a short stroll to see the country's largest 20th-century public building, which opened in 1998. A handsome forecourt fronts the library, whose massive storerooms hold every book published in the UK since 1911.
ⓐ 96 Euston Road ① 020 7412 7000 Ⓦ www.bl.uk ① 09.30–18.00 Mon–Fri, Tues until 20.00, 09.30–17.00 Sat, 11.00–17.00 Sun
Ⓝ King's Cross

British Museum

This stately storehouse of world treasures contains antiquities, artworks and precious objects from around the globe. This is one of the world's great museums, but with thousands of exhibits in over 90 galleries, you won't see it all.

Great Russell Street · 020 7636 1555 or 7323 8299 · www.thebritishmuseum.ac.uk · 10.00–17.30 Sat–Wed, 10.00–20.30 Thur–Fri · Russell Square, Holborn

Cartoon Museum

This museum celebrates the wit and talent of Britain's comic artists. On display are cartoons, caricatures, sketches, letters and original prints, from the 18th century to the present day.

35 Little Russell Street · 020 7580 8155 · www.cartoonmuseum.org · 10.30–17.30 Tues–Sat; admission charge · Holborn, Tottenham Court Road

London Transport Museum

It's not just for kids, but for anyone who's fascinated by the people and vehicles that have kept London moving since the early 19th century.

Covent Garden Piazza · 020 7379 6344 · www.ltmuseum.co.uk · 10.00–18.00; admission charge · Covent Garden · Galleries re-open in spring 2007 after renovation

National Gallery

Behind its neoclassical façade, which stretches along the north side of Trafalgar Square, the National Gallery houses a superlative

---

▶ *The Courtyard of Somerset House is used for concerts during the summer and ice skating in the winter*

collection of Western European art. Among more than 2,300 paintings, dating from 1250 to 1900, are the great artists of every period. Consult a gallery guide and head for your favourites, as you'll never see them all in one go.

ⓐ Trafalgar Square ⓣ 020 7747 2885 ⓦ www.nationalgallery.org.uk ⓛ 10.00–18.00, Wed until 2100 ⓝ Leicester Square, Charing Cross

National Portrait Gallery

Famous and elusive figures from British history are captured on canvas at the National Portrait Gallery, which ranges over three floors in a building behind the National Gallery.

ⓐ St Martin's Place ⓣ 020 7306 0055 ⓦ www.npg.org.uk ⓛ 10.00–18.00 Sat–Wed, 10.00–21.00 Thur & Fri ⓝ Leicester Square

Sir John Soane's Museum

Professor of Architecture at the Royal Academy, Soane converted three townhouses along Lincoln's Inn Fields in the early 19th century to house his quirky collection, and the rambling rooms remain much the same as they were in his day.

ⓐ 13 Lincoln's Inn Fields ⓣ 020 7405 2107 ⓦ www.soane.org ⓛ 10.00–17.00 Tues–Sat; admission charge ⓝ Holborn

Somerset House

Three important art galleries are housed in this handsome Georgian building along the river. Impressionist paintings are the highlight of the Courtauld Gallery, which also has superb works by Rubens and other Old Masters. If it's a hot day, cool off with a splash from the water jets in the courtyard, which turns into an open-air ice rink in the winter.

ⓐ The Strand ⓣ 020 7845 4600 ⓦ www.somerset-house.org.uk ⓛ 10.00–18.00; admission charge ⓝ Temple, Covent Garden

Theatre Museum

The costumes, stage sets and other memorabilia are a big hit with theatre buffs at this museum in Covent Garden's old flower market, which marks the highlights of London's performing arts, from Shakespeare to Shaftesbury Avenue.

ⓐ Russell Street ☎ 020 7943 4700 ⓦ www.theatremuseum.org
🕐 10.00–18.00 Tues–Sun Ⓝ Covent Garden

FOLLOWING IN DICKENS' FOOTSTEPS

No writer has penned a more evocative picture of London than Charles Dickens (1812–70), and, though most of Dickens' London is long gone, you can still visit some of his former haunts. Following his first success with *The Pickwick Papers*, Dickens moved his young family to a handsome house at 48 Doughty Street in 1837. Now the Dickens House Museum, it is the only one of his London homes still standing and is full of memorabilia of his life and works (☎ 020 7405 2127 ⓦ www.dickensmuseum.com 🕐 1000–1700 Mon–Sat, 1100–1700 Sun; admission charge Ⓝ Chancery Lane).
Before he became a writer, Dickens worked as a law clerk at the Inns of Court, the centre of England's legal system since medieval times. You can wander among the quiet courtyards of the four Inns: Gray's Inn where Dickens worked, Inner Temple, Middle Temple and Lincoln's Inn, which Dickens used as the setting for *Bleak House*, recently adapted by the BBC for a popular TV drama.

RETAIL THERAPY

Markets

Stalls selling crafts, jewellery, clothing and accessories operate daily at Covent Garden from around 10.30 until 19.30; on Mondays the market is dedicated to antiques and collectables. For the flavour of an old-time fruit-and-veg market, head for Berwick Street in Soho (🕐 08.00–18.00 Mon–Sat) where barrow boys are hawking produce from their street carts.

Shopping Streets

The stretch of Oxford Street between Oxford Circus and Tottenham Court Road is teeming with young shoppers looking for trendy fashion accessories; for books and music there are large branches of Virgin Megastores, HMV and Borders. It's also the place for kitschy tourist souvenirs. Cobbled Neal Street is Covent Garden's most delightful shopping street, where you can browse through shops selling everything from kites to holistic remedies. Charing Cross Road has long been book-lovers' lane, with many second-hand, specialist and antiquarian shops, particularly in Cecil Court.

Liberty A London institution set in a mock-Tudor building with wooden staircases. Goods range from oriental rugs to Liberty's famous prints. 🏠 210–220 Regent Street 🕐 020 7734 1234 🌐 www.liberty.co.uk 🕐 10.00–18.30 Mon–Fri, until 20.00 Thur, 10.00–19.00 Sat, 12.00–18.00 Sun 🔘 Oxford Circus

The Natural Shoe Store The place for trendy styles and quality brands such as the once-again fashionable Birkenstock, which also has its own store along this street. ⓐ 21 Neal Street ⓣ 020 7836 5254 Ⓦ www.thenaturalshoestore.com Ⓝ Covent Garden

Paul Smith The flagship store of this English designer who creates well-cut clothes for men, women and children. ⓐ 40–44 Floral Street ⓣ 020 7727 3553 Ⓦ www.paulsmith.co.uk Ⓝ Covent Garden

TAKING A BREAK

Bar Italia £ ❶ A pavement table is a must at this trendy Soho café that never goes out of style. Good Italian coffee, pastries and sandwiches. ⓐ 22 Frith Street ⓣ 020 7437 4520 ⓒ 24 hours Mon–Sat, 07.00–04.00 Sun Ⓝ Leicester Square

🔺 *Soho offers a rich array of fun and entertainment*

Food for Thought £ ② Highly popular vegetarian café with a tiny basement dining room and busy takeaway counter. Large portions and low prices. ⓐ 31 Neal Street ⓣ 020 7836 9072 ⓛ 09.30–20.30 Mon–Sat, 12.00–17.00 Sun ⓝ Covent Garden

Punch & Judy £ ③ Brave the crowds for a seat on the balcony overlooking the piazza for the best view of the street performers. Good pub fare. ⓐ Covent Garden Market ⓣ 020 7379 0923 ⓛ 10.00–23.00 Mon–Sat, 12.00–22.30 Sun ⓝ Covent Garden

Patisserie Valerie ££ ④ A Soho institution popular with the arts crowd, serving scrumptious cakes, pastries and coffee as well as light meals. ⓐ 44 Old Compton Street ⓣ 020 7437 3466 ⓛ 07.30–21.00 Mon–Fri, 08.00–21.00 Sat, 09.30–19.00 Sun ⓝ Leicester Square

AFTER DARK

Restaurants
Mildred's £ ⑤ Creative vegetarian fare from stir-fries to veggie burgers is served in stylish Soho surroundings. Great desserts too! No credit cards. ⓐ 45 Lexington Street ⓣ 020 7494 1634 ⓛ noon–23.00 Mon–Sat ⓝ Piccadilly Circus

Rock & Sole Plaice £ ⑥ Fish, not music, is the main attraction at London's oldest fish and chip shop, here since the 1870s. ⓐ 47 Endell Street ⓣ 020 7836 3785 ⓛ 11.30–23.00 Mon–Sat, 12.00–22.00 Sun ⓝ Covent Garden

Wagamama £–££ ⑦ The Bloomsbury location was the first of many canteen-style noodle bars around the city, serving bowls of noodle soups, stir-fries and healthy juice drinks at long, shared tables. Noisy and fun. 4 Streatham Street 020 7323 9223 12.00–23.00 Mon–Sat, 12.30–22.00 Sun Tottenham Court Road

Belgo Centraal ££ Waiters clad in monk's habits serve *moules marinière* by the bucketful, *frites* with mayonnaise, Belgian dishes and a staggering range of Belgian beers in a huge underground restaurant with minimalist decor. 50 Earlham Street, off Neal Street 020 7813 2233 12.00–23.30 Mon–Thur, 12.00–24.00 Fri & Sat, 12.00–22.30 Sun Covent Garden

Mr Kong ££ Of the many great restaurants in Chinatown, locals rate this as one of the best. The Cantonese menu features some unusual dishes and vegetarian specialities. 21 Lisle Street 020 7437 7341 12.00–02.45 Mon–Sat, 12.00–01.45 Sun Leicester Square

Bank ££–£££ There's an uplifting buzz about this big, airy brasserie-style restaurant, which serves contemporary British/international cuisine. Also serves breakfast and weekend brunch. 1 Kingsway 020 7379 9797 07.00–23.30 Mon–Fri, 11.30–23.00 Sat, 11.30–21.30 Sun Covent Garden, Holborn

Hakkasan £££ The ultra-stylish decor in this upmarket Chinese restaurant features an elegant lobby and lattice wood screens in the dining room. From the dim sum lunch platter to beautifully presented main dishes, the food is impeccable. 8 Hanway Place 020 7927 7000 12.00–15.00, 18.00–24.00 Mon–Fri, until 00.30 Thur & Fri, 12.00–16.30, 18.00–00.30 Sat Tottenham Court Road

Mon Plaisir £££ Classic French cuisine and contemporary dishes are served in this pleasant Gallic restaurant, with wood panelling, tiles, abstract paintings and a mirrored bar adding to the continental atmosphere. 🅐 21 Monmouth Street 🕐 020 7836 7243 🕒 12.00–15.00, 17.45–24.00 Mon–Fri, 12.00–15.00 Sat Ⓝ Covent Garden

Pearl £££ Set in a marble dining room adorned with over a million hand-strung pearls, Pearl is one of the most glamorous restaurants in the capital. The modern French cuisine is complemented by fine wines, over 50 available by the glass. Start with a drink from the champagne trolley in the elegant front bar. 🅐 252 High Holborn 🕐 020 7829 7000 Ⓦ www.pearl-restaurant.com 🕒 12.00–14.30 Mon–Fri, 18.00–22.00 Mon–Sat Ⓝ Holborn

Cinemas & Theatres
Donmar Warehouse Several Hollywood stars have tread the boards at this Off-West End theatre, known for producing new plays and fresh takes on the classics. 🅐 41 Earlham Street 🕐 0870 060 6624 Ⓦ www.donmarwarehouse.com Ⓝ Covent Garden, Leicester Square

London Coliseum Productions of the English National Opera here are staged in English. 🅐 St Martin's Lane 🕐 020 7632 8300 Ⓦ www.eno.org Ⓝ Leicester Square, Charing Cross

Royal Opera House In addition to its classic opera productions, London's beautiful world-class opera house is home to the Royal

---

❿ *Street entertainers captivate audiences in Covent Garden*

Ballet. Bow Street 020 7304 4000 www.royaloperahouse.org
 Covent Garden

Soho Theatre New playwrights find an outlet at this no-frills, Off-West End venue, which also features late-night shows, comedy acts and a cool café. 21 Dean Street 0870 429 6883
 www.sohotheatre.com Tottenham Court Road

West End Theatre District More than 50 theatres are clustered between the bottom end of Tottenham Court Road and Charing Cross, from Covent Garden to Piccadilly Circus. Productions range from popular musicals to dramas featuring major film stars. Check the listings in the national newspapers and *Time Out* for current offerings.

Bars, Clubs & Discos

Bar Rumba This Soho basement club is a firm favourite on the club circuit, with regular theme nights including Barrio Latino on Tuesdays and the Movement drum-and-bass on Thursdays.
 36 Shaftesbury Avenue 020 7287 6933 www.barrumba.co.uk
 21.00–03.00 Mon & Wed, 18.00–03.00 Tues, Thur & Fri, 21.00–04.00 Sat, 20.00–02.00 Sun Piccadilly Circus

Floridita Terence Conran's chic cocktail bar, inspired by the Cuban original, offers exotic drink concoctions and a house band.
 100 Wardour Street 020 7314 4000 www.floriditalondon.com
 17.30–02.00 Mon–Wed, 17.30–03.00 Thur–Sat Leicester Square, Tottenham Court Road

Heaven London's best-known gay club has turned 25 and the party's still going strong. Top nights at this huge venue, under the arches in Villiers Street, are Mondays (Popcorn), Wednesdays (Fruit Machine) and Saturdays (Heaven), with top DJs and shows. ⓐ Villiers Street ⓣ 020 7930 2020 ⓦ www.heaven-london.com ⓛ 22.30–03.00 Mon, 22.30–06.00 Wed, 22.00–06.00 Fri & Sat ⓝ Charing Cross, Embankment

Madame Jo Jo's The cabaret-style dance venue recalls the days of Soho sleaze, the music ranges from Deep Funk (Fridays) to White Heat's (Tuesdays) punk and indie sounds. ⓐ 8 Brewer Street ⓣ 020 7734 3040 ⓦ www.madamejojos.com ⓛ 20.00–03.00 Tues, 22.00–03.00 Wed & Fri, 21.00–03.00 Thur, 19.00–03.00 Sat, 22.00–02.00 Sun ⓝ Leicester Square, Piccadilly Circus

The Salisbury Arguably the capital's most beautiful Victorian pub, with etched glass windows and an ornate interior, it's popular with patrons from the nearby theatres. ⓐ 90 St Martin's Lane ⓣ 020 7836 5863 ⓛ 11.00–24.00 Mon–Fri, 12.00–23.00 Sat, 12.00–22.30 Sun ⓝ Leicester Square

Water Rats Indie and alternative rock bands take to the well-worn stage, hoping to make it big like Oasis and Bob Dylan, who played their first London gigs here. ⓐ 328 Grays Inn Road ⓣ 020 7837 7269 ⓦ www.plummusic.com ⓛ 19.30–23.00 (music) Mon–Sat ⓝ King's Cross

Central London 2

WESTMINSTER TO MARYLEBONE

Several of London's most venerable landmarks can be found in Westminster, the seat of government and monarchy since medieval times. When you've tired of the pomp and circumstance, wander north into Mayfair and Marylebone for some retail therapy in the capital's best-known shopping streets and department stores. Sightseeing in Westminster is best done on foot, and on a fine day Green Park and St James's Park make a refreshing break between activities.

SIGHTS & ATTRACTIONS

Buckingham Palace

London's most famous des res may not be the city's prettiest building, but it's home to the Queen. When she's away in August and September, you can visit, for a price, the magnificent State Rooms and Picture Gallery to see the sumptuous furnishings. At other times, you'll have to be content with peering through the gilded gates.

ⓐ Buckingham Gate ⓣ 020 7766 7300 ⓦ www.royalresidences.com ⓛ 09.30–16.15 Aug–Sept; Changing of the Guard 11.00, daily in summer, alternate days in winter; admission charge ⓜ Victoria, Green Park ⓘ Queues can be long, so it's best to book a timed ticket in advance

Cabinet War Rooms

A fascinating part of London's history is kept alive 3 m (9 ft) below ground, in the warren of rooms where Churchill and the War Cabinet

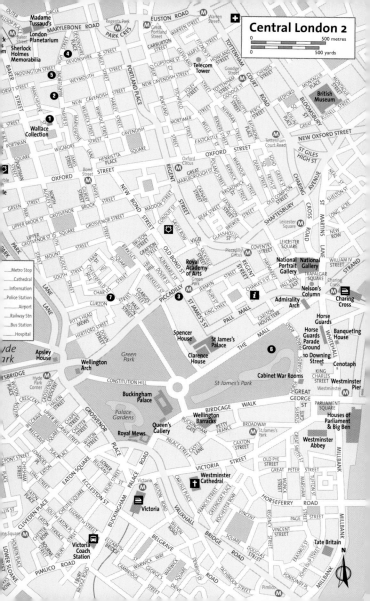

Central London 2

0 — 500 metres
0 — 500 yards

Map Legend

..... Metro Stop
... Cathedral
... Information
... Police Station
..... Airport
..... Railway Stn
..... Bus Station
..... Hospital

Labelled Locations

Madame Tussaud's
London Planetarium
Sherlock Holmes Memorabilia
Wallace Collection
Telecom Tower
British Museum
Regents Park
PARK CRES.
Oxford Circus
Piccadilly Circus
Royal Academy of Arts
National Portrait Gallery
National Gallery
Nelson's Column
Admiralty Arch
Leicester Square
Charing Cross
Horse Guards
Horse Guards Parade Ground
Banqueting House
Spencer House
St James's Palace
Clarence House
Cabinet War Rooms
to Downing Street
Cenotaph
Westminster Pier
Apsley House
Wellington Arch
Green Park
St James's Park
Buckingham Palace
Palace Gardens
Wellington Barracks
Queen's Gallery
Royal Mews
Great George St
Houses of Parliament & Big Ben
Westminster Abbey
Westminster Cathedral
Victoria
Victoria Coach Station
Tate Britain

Street Names

OUTER CIRCLE
ALLSOP PLACE
EUSTON ROAD
Warren Street
Baker Street
MARYLEBONE ROAD
Great Portland Street
CARBURTON ST.
CLIPSTONE ST.
Regent's Park
PADDINGTON STREET
DEVONSHIRE
WEYMOUTH STREET
NEW CAVENDISH STREET
PORTLAND PLACE
MORTIMER STREET
TOTTENHAM COURT ROAD
Goodge Street
CHENIES ST.
MONTAGUE PLACE
RUSSELL SQ.
BLOOMSBURY
MONTAGUE ST.
GREAT RUSSELL
DORSET STREET
MANCHESTER STREET
HARLEY STREET
WIMPOLE STREET
PORTLAND PLACE
GREAT PORTLAND STREET
NEW OXFORD STREET
ST GILES HIGH ST
WIGMORE STREET
HENRIETTA PLACE
CAVENDISH SQUARE
OXFORD CIRCUS
GREAT MARLBOROUGH ST.
SHAFTESBURY
PORTMAN
OXFORD STREET
OXFORD STREET
NEW BOND STREET
REGENT STREET
CARNABY
SHAFTESBURY
CHARING CROSS ROAD
NEAL ST
SHELTON ST
LONG ACRE
NEW ROW
NORTH AUDLEY ST
GILBERT STREET
BROOK STREET
MADDOX STREET
CONDUIT ST
SAVILE ROW
BEAK ST
BREWER STREET
OLD COMPTON ST
UPPER BROOK ST
GROSVENOR STREET
GROSVENOR SQUARE
UPPER GROSVENOR ST
MOUNT STREET
SOUTH STREET
BERKELEY SQUARE
BRUTON STREET
GRAFTON ST
DOVER ST
ALBEMARLE ST
OLD BOND ST
VIGO
GLASSHOUSE ST
REGENT ST
COVENTRY ST
LEICESTER SQUARE
WILLIAM IV STREET
STRAND
PARK LANE
CHESTERFIELD HILL
CHARLES STREET
CURZON STREET
BERKELEY ST
PICCADILLY
JERMYN ST
ST JAMES'S ST
CHARLES II ST
PALL MALL
CARLTON HOUSE TERRACE
WHITEHALL
PITT'S HEAD MEWS
HERTFORD STREET
DOWN STREET
Green Park
THE MALL
KING STREET
KING CHARLES STREET
GREAT GEORGE STREET
PARLIAMENT SQUARE
HYDE PARK CORNER
CONSTITUTION HILL
BIRDCAGE WALK
STOREY'S GATE
KNIGHTSBRIDGE
WILTON PLACE
GROSVENOR CRESCENT
UPPER BELGRAVE STREET
CHAPEL STREET
GROSVENOR PLACE
BUCKINGHAM GATE
PETTY FRANCE
BROADWAY
St James's Park
CAXTON STREET
OLD PYE STREET
GREAT PETER STREET
MILLBANK
BELGRAVE SQUARE
CHESTER STREET
WILTON STREET
LOWER BELGRAVE ST
PALACE STREET
CASTLE LANE
VICTORIA
VICTORIA STREET
FRANCIS ST
GREENCOAT ROW
ROCHESTER ROW
MONCK STREET
MARSHAM STREET
TUFTON STREET
PONT STREET
CHESHAM PLACE
EATON SQUARE
EATON PLACE
CHESTER SQUARE
ELIZABETH ST
EBURY STREET
BUCKINGHAM PALACE ROAD
WILTON ROAD
CAUSTON PLACE
VINCENT SQUARE
REGENCY STREET
PAGE ST
HORSEFERRY ROAD
LOWER SLOANE
CLIVEDEN PLACE
EATON TERRACE
SOUTH EATON PLACE
CHESTER ROW
EBURY STREET
SEMLEY PLACE
ELIZABETH BRIDGE
WARWICK WAY
GEORGE'S DRIVE
CAMBRIDGE STREET
DENBIGH ST
TACHBROOK STREET
VINCENT STREET
VAUXHALL BRIDGE ROAD
PIMLICO ROAD
EBURY BRIDGE ROAD
LUPUS STREET
GROSVENOR ROAD
PONSONBY PL
MILLBANK
Pimlico
MILLBANK

N

directed operations during the bombing raids of World War II. There
is also a museum commemorating Churchill's life and times.

ⓐ Clive Steps, King Charles Street ⓣ 020 7930 6961
ⓦ www.iwm.org.uk ⓛ 09.30–18.00; admission charge Ⓝ Westminster

Houses of Parliament & Big Ben

Though Westminster has been the site of government since 1265,
today's Houses of Parliament are relatively recent, designed by
Charles Barry and Augustus Pugin to replace the medieval palace
that burned down in 1834. Their Victorian Gothic building, covering
3 hectares (7.4 acres) and stretching 266 m (873 ft) along the
Thames, is today one of London's most famous façades. The clock
tower, which houses the 13.5-tonne bell named Big Ben, is a London
icon, as is the bell's hourly chime.

ⓐ Parliament Square ⓣ 020 7219 3000 ⓦ www.parliament.uk
Ⓝ Westminster

Madame Tussaud's

The real Madame Tussaud introduced Londoners to her waxwork
figures over 200 years ago, and today they're one of the most
popular attractions in the capital. Exhibits include leading film,
music and sports stars, royalty and world leaders, and the ghoulish
Chamber of Horrors.

ⓐ Marylebone Road ⓣ 0870 400 3000 ⓦ www.madame-
tussauds.com ⓛ 09.30–17.30 Mon–Fri, 09.00–18.00 Sat & Sun;
admission charge Ⓝ Baker Street

Marble Arch

Designed by John Nash in 1828, this white marble monument was
meant to be the gateway to Buckingham Palace. But it proved too

narrow for the passage of state coaches and was moved to the northeast corner of Hyde Park, where it stands forlornly on a busy traffic island. Ⓝ Marble Arch

Royal Mews

If you're a lover of horses or fairytales, a visit to the Royal Mews is a treat. The stables house the royal carriages and horses, including the Windsor greys that pull the 4-tonne gold state coach, built in 1762 and used for coronations ever since. You can also see the glass coach that carried Princess Diana on her wedding day.
Ⓐ Buckingham Palace Road Ⓣ 020 7766 7302
Ⓦ www.royalresidences.com Ⓛ 11.00–16.00 Mon–Thur (Mar–July, Oct); 10.00–17.00 (Aug–Sept) Ⓝ Victoria

Spencer House

Built in the 18th-century, this Palladian mansion was the ancestral home of Diana, Princess of Wales and is the finest of its era in London. You can tour several of the opulent interior rooms, restored to their former glory by the present owners, the Rothschilds.
Ⓐ 27 St James's Place Ⓣ 020 7499 8620 Ⓦ www.spencerhouse.co.uk
Ⓛ 10.30–17.45 Sun, closed Jan, Aug; admission charge
Ⓝ Green Park

St James's Park

You'd be hard-pressed to find a lovelier spot to chill out from the city's excesses than this former royal deer park. Charles II landscaped it and opened it to the public, and used to stroll here with his mistresses. At one end of the narrow central lake is Duck Island, which harbours black swans, geese, waterfowl and pelicans, a legacy of the king's original bird sanctuary.

Thames River Cruise

The Thames flows through the heart of London, and one of the best ways to see the city sights is on a river cruise. Several companies offer cruises from various departure points, but Westminster Pier is a good central point with several options. From here you can go upriver to Kew Gardens and Hampton Court, or downriver to Greenwich and all the way to the Thames Barrier. For shorter trips, the cruise between Westminster Pier and Tower Bridge is highly recommended. The 25-minute trip passes highlights such as the Millennium Bridge, St Paul's and the Globe Theatre, along with a lively commentary. The tourist office has a list of operators, or contact City Cruises.
🛈 020 7740 0400 Ⓝ Westminster

Westminster Abbey

As much a national monument as a house of worship, Westminster Abbey has been the coronation site and burial place of English monarchs since 1066. It contains some of the finest medieval architecture in London, from the soaring, French Gothic nave to the beautiful Lady Chapel and octagonal Chapter House.
ⓐ Parliament Square 🛈 020 7222 5152 Ⓦ www.westminster-abbey.org 🕐 09.30–15.45 (last admission) Mon–Fri, 09.30–13.45 Sat, Sun services only; admission charge Ⓝ Westminster

CULTURE

Queen's Gallery

Rotating exhibits from the spectacular art collection amassed by British royalty over the past few hundred years are displayed in a rebuilt chapel at the west end of Buckingham Palace.
ⓐ Buckingham Palace Road 🛈 020 7766 7301

Ⓦ www.the-royal-collection.org.uk or Ⓦ www.royalresidences.com
Ⓛ 09.30–17.00 25 July–24 Sept; 10.00–17.30 rest of the year;
admission charge Ⓝ Victoria, Green Park

Royal Academy of Arts

Some of the capital's most impressive international exhibitions are
staged here in Burlington House, home of the Royal Academy of
Arts which was founded in the 18th century as the nation's first
formal art school. The highlight of the permanent collection is
Michelangelo's marble *Virgin and Child with the Infant St John*,
one of only four of his sculptures outside Italy.
ⓐ Piccadilly Ⓣ 020 7300 5760 Ⓦ www.royalacademy.org.uk
Ⓛ 10.00–18.00, until 22.00 Fri; admission charge
Ⓝ Piccadilly Circus

🔺 *Travelling by boat will afford you unique views of the city's skyline*

Tate Britain

The former Tate Gallery is now devoted exclusively to British art from 1500 to the present day. Only a fraction of its huge collection is on show and paintings are rotated every year, featuring works by such artists as Hogarth and Constable, as well as contemporary names.
🄰 Millbank 🄲 020 7887 8000 🅦 www.tate.org.uk 🄻 10.00–17.50
🄽 Pimlico

A ROYAL WALK

This area is the heart of Royal London and the centre of British government. To see the highlights, walk up The Mall from Buckingham Palace. This broad thoroughfare which borders St James Park is used for state processions and ends at Trafalgar Square. You'll pass Clarence House, London home of Prince Charles, and St James's Palace, the official court. At the top is Admiralty Arch – the central arch is reserved for the monarch. Look right down Horse Guards Parade, where annual pageants such as Trooping the Colour take place.

Turn right and walk down Whitehall. Past the Admiralty building is the entrance to Horse Guards, where two straight-faced troopers mounted on horseback keep the traditional guard (🄻 10.00–17.00 Mon–Sat).

Next you'll pass the official residence of the prime minister, behind the gates, at 10 Downing Street. Ahead is the Cenotaph, a memorial to those who gave their lives in both world wars. Turn right on King Charles Street to return to Green Park. Further along Bird Cage Walk, named for Charles II's menagerie, is Wellington Barracks where the band musters for the Changing of the Guard.

Wallace Collection

The small but superb private art collection amassed by the Hertford family in the 19th century is exquisitely displayed in their former mansion. It ranges from Sevres porcelain and French furniture to paintings by Rembrandt, Hals, Titian and others.

ⓐ Hertford House, Manchester Square ⓣ 020 7563 9500
ⓦ www.wallacecollection.org ⓛ 10.00–17.00 ⓝ Bond Street

🔺 *A solemn protector: the Queen's Guard on horseback*

RETAIL THERAPY

Shopping Streets & Markets

Many of London's biggest department stores line up along the stretch of Oxford Street between Oxford Circus and Marble Arch. Bond Street, synonymous with upmarket shopping, runs between Oxford Street and Piccadilly with many designer label clothes shops and top jewellers like Tiffany and Asprey. Burlington Arcade off Piccadilly is a covered block of fine merchandise behind lovely 19th-century shopfronts, watched over by top-hatted, frock-coated beadles. Jermyn Street is another step back in time with centuries-old shops. Marylebone High Street still has the kind of one-off shops and boutiques that are fast disappearing as chain stores take over London. A charming market is set up in the courtyard of St James's Church, Piccadilly, selling antiques on Tuesday (🕒 10.00–18.00) and arts and crafts Wednesday–Saturday (10.00–18.00).

Brown's Cutting-edge fashions for men and women from a great range of designers, well-known and up-and-coming. If you're on a budget, head for Brown's Labels for Less at No. 50. 🏠 23–27 South Molton Street 📞 020 7514 0000 🌐 www.brownsfashions.com 🕒 10.00–18.30 Mon–Sat, until 19.00 Thur 🚇 Bond Street

Fortnum & Mason Marble pillars, wood paneling and chandeliers deck the food halls of this landmark. This is the place for top-notch foodie treats and gifts, and there's a fine perfumery and accessories department too. 🏠 Piccadilly 📞 020 7734 8040 🌐 www.fortnumandmason.co.uk 🕒 10.00–18.30 Mon–Sat, 12.00–18.00 Sun 🚇 Green Park, Piccadilly Circus

Grays Antique Market With stalls selling everything from jewellery and silver to art deco paperweights and toys, this is a great place to browse for unique gifts. ⓐ 58 Davies Street ⓣ 020 7629 7034 ⓦ www.graysantiques.com ⓛ 10.00–18.00 Mon–Fri ⓜ Bond Street

Selfridges The grande dame of London department stores has everything from top designer labels to trendy fashions, a sprawling cosmetics section, food halls, restaurants and even a champagne bar. ⓐ 400 Oxford Street ⓣ 0870 837 7377 ⓦ www.selfridges.com ⓛ 09.30–20.00 Mon–Fri, 09.30–20.00 Sat, 11.30–18.00 Sun ⓜ Bond Street, Marble Arch

Waterstones This well-known chain turned the old Simpson's department store into Europe's biggest bookshop, with five floors of titles covering every subject under the sun. ⓐ 203–206 Piccadilly ⓣ 020 7851 2400 ⓦ www.waterstones.co.uk ⓛ 10.00–22.00 Mon–Sat, 12.00–18.00 Sun ⓜ Piccadilly Circus

△ *Shoppers' paradise at Selfridges, in Oxford Street*

TAKING A BREAK

Café Bagatelle £–££ ❶ Located in the glass-roofed sculpture garden of Hertford House, the Wallace Collection's museum restaurant is a delightful spot for a cup of tea or a light meal of European fare with Asian touches. ⓐ Manchester Square ⓣ 020 7563 0505 ⓛ 10.00–17.00 ⓝ Bond Street

Patisserie Valerie at Sagne £–££ ❷ A 1920s decor combined with delectable delights. ⓐ 105 Marylebone High Street ⓣ 020 7935 6240 ⓛ 07.30–19.00 Mon–Fri, 08.00–19.00 Sat, 09.00–18.00 Sun ⓝ Bond Street

The Wolseley £–££ ❸ The 1920s decor of this former automobile showroom makes a classy stop for breakfast, afternoon tea or a snack. ⓐ 160 Piccadilly ⓣ 020 7499 6996 ⓦ www.thewolseley.com ⓛ 07.00–24.00 Mon–Fri, 11.30–24.00 Sat, 11.30–23.00 Sun ⓝ Green Park

AFTER DARK

Restaurants
Eat & Two Veg £ ❹ The mix of Greek, Thai and Italian dishes on the menu makes this bustling vegetarian restaurant a cut above the usual fare. ⓐ 50 Marylebone High Street ⓣ 020 7258 8595 ⓛ 09.00–23.00 Mon–Sat, 10.00–22.00 Sun ⓝ Bond Street

La Galette £–££ ❺ Galettes are French buckwheat pancakes with savoury or sweet fillings – a great way to dine on French cuisine without the fuss. ⓐ 56 Paddington Street ⓣ 020 7935 1554

Ⓦ www.lagalette.com Ⓛ 09.30–23.00 Mon–Fri, 10.00–23.00 Sat & Sun Ⓝ Baker Street

Inn the Park ££ ❻ Fabulous location overlooking the lake and Duck Island in St James's Park, and excellent British food using fresh seasonal produce from small producers. Ⓐ St James's Park Ⓣ 020 7451 9999 Ⓦ www.innthepark.co.uk Ⓛ 08.00–11.00, 12.00–15.00, 18.00–22.30 Mon–Fri, 09.00–11.00, 12.00–16.00, 18.00–22.30 Sat & Sun Ⓝ St James's Park

Tamarind £££ ❼ Mogul tandoori cuisine is the speciality at the only Michelin Star Indian restaurant in the country. Ⓐ 20 Queen Street Ⓣ 020 7629 3561 Ⓦ www.tamarindrestaurant.com Ⓛ 12.00–15.00, 18.00–23.30 Mon–Fri, 18.00–23.30 Sat, 12.00–14.30, 18.00–22.30 Sun

Bars, Clubs & Discos
Red Lion This classic Westminster pub near the Houses of Parliament has a division bell that summons MPs to votes. Ⓐ 48 Parliament Street Ⓣ 020 7930 5826 Ⓛ 11.00–23.00 Mon–Fri, 11.00–09.30 Sat, 12.00–19.00 Sun Ⓝ Westminster

The Social Trendy alternative rockers and people in the music business frequent this Marylebone DJ bar. Ⓐ 5 Little Portland Street Ⓣ 020 7636 4992 Ⓦ www.thesocial.com Ⓛ 12.00–24.00 Mon–Fri, 13.00–24.00 Sat Ⓝ Oxford Circus

Ye Grapes A good range of beers is on offer at this charming Victorian pub, tucked away on a pleasant little square in Mayfair. Ⓐ 16 Shepherd Market Ⓛ 11.00–23.00 Ⓝ Green Park

West London

West London is generally well-heeled, encompassing the upmarket shopping and residential areas of Knightsbridge, Kensington and Sloane Square. But there's also the trendier, funkier quarters of Notting Hill and Chelsea's King's Road. The green expanse of Hyde Park and Kensington Gardens is a great place to shake off urban stress. While three of London's top museums stand conveniently side by side in South Kensington, the Tube is often the quickest way to get between the attractions and areas recommended here.

SIGHTS & ATTRACTIONS

Chelsea

There are two sides to Chelsea; the fun and funky King's Road where Swinging '60s fashion and punk was born, and the handsome homes and walled gardens of the leafy streets that attracted many 19th-century writers and artists. Chelsea is less bohemian and more upmarket today. But it's still worth a stroll down the King's Road, browsing in the boutiques and posing in the cosmopolitan cafés, or following the trail of blue plaques through the side streets to Cheyne Walk, which counts Mick Jagger (No 48) and Keith Richards (No 3) among the famous names who once lived here.

Chelsea Physic Garden

Britain's second-oldest botanical garden, founded in 1673 by the Royal Society of Apothecaries for the study of medicinal plants, is a delight for serious gardeners. The garden is still used for research, and there are displays of edible flowers and herbs, poisonous plants and various useful species.

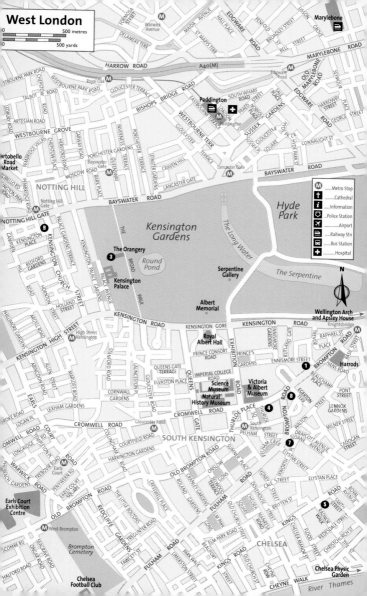

ⓐ 66 Royal Hospital Road ☎ 020 7352 5646
ⓦ www.chelseaphysicgarden.co.uk 🕐 12.00–17.00 Wed, 14.00–18.00
Sun, Apr–Oct; admission charge Ⓜ Sloane Square

Harrods

Whether or not you buy anything, London's landmark department
store is an attraction in its own right. Spreading over seven floors
and several acres, it lives up to its motto: 'everything for everyone,
everywhere' (though at a price). The highlight is the Food Hall,
with its Arts and Crafts tiling and every gourmet temptation
under the sun.
ⓐ Brompton Road, Knightsbridge ☎ 020 7730 1234
ⓦ www.harrods.com 🕐 10.00–20.00 Mon–Sat, Sun 12.00–18.00
Ⓜ Knightsbridge

Hyde Park

One thing that sets London apart from other cities is the healthy
amount of green space in the city centre. The largest is Hyde Park,
which, together with the adjoining Kensington Gardens, stretches a
mile and a half east to west. It's criss-crossed by paths for walking,
running and biking, and you can hire boats for paddling about on the
Serpentine, the central artificial lake. Take in the free art exhibitions
at the little Serpentine Gallery on the west side. At the northeast
corner is the famous Speakers' Corner, where earnest eccentrics air
their views and battle the hecklers every Sunday morning. Political
demonstrations have also taken place here, the largest was in 2003
when more than a million people came to protest against the
coming war in Iraq. But these days the huge crowds are more likely
to be heading for the occasional mass concerts held in the park,
featuring everyone from rock stars to Pavarotti.

Kensington Gardens

Formerly the grounds for Kensington Palace, these pretty gardens became a public park in the mid-19th century. The round pond is a popular spot for roller-skaters and for sailing model boats. At the tail of the Serpentine, known as the Long Water, are the Italian Gardens with five fountains. Nearby is the beloved statue of Peter Pan, erected by the book's author JM Barrie, who met the young family who inspired his story here. Another favourite with children is the Princess Diana Memorial Playground in the park's north-west corner.

Kensington Palace

The palace, which borders the west end of Kensington Gardens, was the home of Diana, Princess of Wales after her marriage to Prince Charles until her death in 1997. The royal apartments, where some members of the royal family live, are private, but the 18th-century state rooms are open to the public. Afterwards, visit the lovely Sunken Garden and the Orangery where you can have refreshments. ⓐ entrance from Broad Walk, Kensington Gardens ⓣ 020 7937 9561 ⓦ www.hrp.org.uk ⓛ 10.00–18.00, 17.00 in winter; admission charge ⓝ High Street Kensington, Queensway

Wellington Arch

In the south-east corner of Hyde Park, opposite his former residence, this neoclassical monument celebrates the Duke of Wellington's victories in the Napoleonic wars. Inside is a small exhibition about London's memorials and statues, but the best reason to visit is for the views from the top of the arch over the surrounding scene. ⓐ Hyde Park Corner ⓣ 020 7973 2726 ⓦ www.english-heritage.org.uk ⓛ 10.00–17.00 Wed–Sun, Apr–Oct; until 16.00 Nov–Mar; admission charge ⓝ Hyde Park Corner

CULTURE

Apsley House

Arthur Wellesley, the 1st Duke of Wellington, moved into this 18th-century mansion – then known as No 1, London – following his victory over Napoleon at Waterloo in 1815. Although his descendants still live here, most of the house is used to display the Duke's superlative art collection. Many pieces were gifts from European royals in gratitude for Napoleon's defeat.

149 Piccadilly, Hyde Park Corner 020 7499 5676 www.english-heritage.org.uk 10.00–17.00 Tues–Sun, Apr–Oct; 10.00–16.00 Tues–Sun, Nov–Mar; admission charge Hyde Park Corner

Natural History Museum

The cathedral-like central hall of this much-loved museum is a perfect home for the life-size dinosaur skeletons and animated models. Explore the Earth Galleries, where you can experience a simulated earthquake, the new Darwin Wing, and exhibits on ecology, gemstones and creepy-crawlies.

Cromwell Road 020 7942 5000 www.nhm.ac.uk 10.00–17.50 Mon–Sat, 11.00–17.50 Sun South Kensington

Science Museum

Full of fascinating and entertaining exhibits that explain the mysteries of science, this huge museum appeals to adults and children alike. With more than 200,000 exhibits spread over seven floors, it can be exhausting, so grab a floor plan and head for a topic that most appeals.

Exhibition Road 0870 870 4868 www.sciencemuseum.org.uk 10.00–18.00 Mon–Sun South Kensington

Victoria & Albert Museum

The museum founded by Prince Albert in 1852 to inspire excellence in British manufacturing and design has grown into the greatest collection of decorative arts in the world. Winding through 11 km (7 miles) are galleries filled with priceless objects from around the world.

ⓐ Cromwell Road ⓣ 020 7942 2000 ⓦ www.vam.ac.uk

ⓛ 10.00–17.45, Wed until 22.00 and last Fri of the month

ⓝ South Kensington

🔺 *Ancient dinosaurs live on at the Natural History Museum*

95

RETAIL THERAPY

Shopping Streets & Markets

Notting Hill's Portobello Road is one of the most famous street markets in London. It's known for its antiques, but you'll also find vintage clothing, bric-a-brac and food (🕐 08.00–19.00 Mon–Wed & Sat, 08.00–13.00 Thur, 08.00–18.00 Fri). Chelsea's King's Road, synonymous with avante-garde fashions since the 1960s, is tamer these days but you'll still find some funky boutiques amidst the upmarket interiors and children's wear shops. For designer labels, head for Knightsbridge, where top names cluster around Brompton Road, Sloane Avenue and Fulham Road. Along Kensington Church Street, shop for everything from antiques to second-hand designer bargains.

Agent Provocateur With its glam undergarments ranging from naughty to nice, this shop will seduce you with its sexy shoes and lingerie. 🅐 16 Pont Street 🅣 020 7235 0229 🅦 www.agentprovocateur.com 🕐 10.00–18.00 Mon–Sat 🅝 Knightsbridge, Sloane Square

Books for Cooks Tomes of culinary inspiration line the shelves at this Notting Hill favourite, with new and second-hand books dedicated to every food, cuisine and cookery method under the sun. 🅐 4 Blenheim Crescent 🅣 020 7221 1992 🅦 www.booksforcooks.com 🕐 10.00–18.00 Tues–Sat 🅝 Ladbroke Grove

Cath Kidston The homewares designer's floral, striped and polka-dot prints are slightly retro and decorate everything from pillows to

▶ *The Albert Memorial sits proudly at the edge of Hyde Park*

lamps and bed linen. ⓐ 8 Clarendon Cross ❶ 020 7221 4000
ⓦ www.cathkidston.co.uk ❶ 10.00–18.00 Mon–Sat, 12.00–17.00 Sun
ⓝ Holland Park

Harvey Nichols From its hip beauty bar with all the latest skin
care and make-up products to its fabulous fashions and exquisite
home furnishings, this perennially cool department store has it all.
ⓐ 67 Brompton Road ❶ 020 7235 5000 ⓦ www.harveynichols.com
❶ 10.00–19.00 Mon–Tues & Sat, 10.00–20.00 Wed–Fri, 12.00–18.00
Sun ⓝ Knightsbridge

Space NK The latest in cosmetics, fragrances, skin care and
perfumed candles are sold at this flagship Notting Hill store, which
also has a spa, and other locations in the city. ⓐ 127–131 Westbourne
Grove ❶ 020 7727 8063 ⓦ www.spacenk.co.uk ❶ 11.00–19.00 Mon,
10.00–19.00 Tues, Fri & Sat, 10.00–20.00 Wed–Thur, 12.00–18.00 Sun
ⓝ Notting Hill

TAKING A BREAK

Gloriette £ ❶ Scrumptious cakes and good coffee draw tired
shoppers to this Viennese café, long a fixture on the Knightsbridge
scene. Light meals are also served. ⓐ 1128 Brompton Road ❶ 020 7589
4635 ❶ 07.00–20.00 Mon–Fri, 08.00–20.00 Sat, 09.00–18.00 Sun
ⓝ Knightsbridge

Hummingbird Bakery £ ❷ Pavement tables make this delightful
little place a great spot for people-watching too, while munching on

◀ *Houses in Chelsea sell for around £1 million*

its cupcakes, muffins and other American-style baked goods.
ⓐ 133 Portobello Road ⓣ 020 7229 6446 ⓛ 10.00–18.00 Mon–Sat,
11.00–18.00 Sun ⓝ Notting Hill

The Orangery £ ❸ There's no better place for a cup of good tea –
and a cake or savoury tart – than Hawksmoor's lovely Orangery, built
for Queen Anne in the grounds of Kensington Palace. ⓐ Kensington
Gardens ⓣ 020 7376 0239 ⓛ 10.00–18.00 Mar–Oct, 10.00–17.00
Nov–Feb ⓝ Queensway

Orsini's Café £ ❹ This authentic Italian café opposite the V&A
serves wonderful cappuccino, great pastas and daily specials.
ⓐ 8a Thurloe Place ⓣ 020 7581 5553 ⓛ Breakfast, lunch, dinner daily
ⓝ South Kensington

AFTER DARK

Restaurants
Chelsea Kitchen £ ❺ One of the few bargain eating spots in this
part of London, this long-standing local favourite has cheap-and-
cheerful café fare. ⓐ 98 Kings Road ⓣ 020 7589 1330 ⓛ 08.00–23.30
Mon–Sat, 09.00–23.30 Sun ⓝ Sloane Square

Osteria Basilico ££ ❻ Wonderfully authentic Italian fare, from
pizza and pasta to meat and fish dishes, are served at this attractive
restaurant near Portobello Road. ⓐ 29 Kensington Park Road ⓣ 020
7727 9372 ⓛ 12.30–15.00, until 16.00 Sat, 18.30–23.00 Mon–Sat,
12.30–15.30, 18.30–22.30 Sun ⓝ Notting Hill Gate

ⓞ *Simpsons in the Strand is great for those with larger budgets*

Bibendum ££–£££ ❼ The Art Nouveau decor of tiles and stained glass at Michelin House is reason enough to come, but the food and wine are superb as well. If you're watching the budget, the three-course prix fixe menu (under £30) or the Oyster Bar (open all day) are great value. Ⓐ 81 Fulham Road Ⓣ 020 7581 5817 Ⓦ www.bibendum.co.uk Ⓖ 12.00–14.30, 19.00–23.30 Mon–Fri, 12.30–15.00, 19.00–23.30 Sat, 12.30–15.00, 19.00–22.30 Sun Ⓝ South Kensington

Racine ££–£££ ❽ Traditional French cooking in elegant surroundings and friendly service makes this Knightsbridge restaurant highly popular, so book ahead. Ⓐ 239 Brompton Road Ⓣ 020 7584 4477 Ⓖ 12.00–15.00, 18.00–22.30 Mon–Fri, 12.00–15.30, 18.00–22.30 Sat, 12.00–15.30, 18.00–22.00 Sun Ⓝ Knightsbridge, South Kensington

Kensington Place £££ ❾ The see-and-be-seen, open-plan dining room is always buzzing at this fashionable restaurant, which serves excellent, unfussy modern British/international cuisine. Ⓐ 201–209 Kensington Church Street Ⓣ 020 7727 3184 Ⓖ 12.00–15.30, 18.30–23.45 Mon–Sat, 12.00–15.30, 18.30–22.15 Sun Ⓝ Notting Hill Gate

Cinemas & Theatres
Royal Albert Hall Built in the round, this grand Victorian concert hall is the venue for large shows, from rock and jazz to classical music, and is the home of the Proms concert series every summer. Ⓐ Kensington Gore Ⓣ 020 7589 3203 Ⓦ www.royalalberthall.com Ⓝ South Kensington

Royal Court Theatre From its prime position on Sloane Square, this 50-year-old theatre continues its acclaimed productions of new work by established and emerging playwrights. ⓐ Sloane Square ⓣ 020 7565 5000 ⓦ www.royalcourttheatre.com ⓝ Sloane Square

Bars, Clubs & Discos

Admiral Codrington The Cod is an old Chelsea favourite turned gastro-pub. The outdoor tables are the place to be on fine summer evenings. ⓐ 17 Mossop Street ⓣ 020 7581 0005 ⓛ 11.30–23.00 Mon–Sat, 12.00–22.30 Sun ⓝ South Kensington

Cherry Jam This stylish underground cocktail bar features top London DJs, including owner Ben Watt of Everything But the Girl fame. ⓐ 52 Porchester Road ⓣ 020 7720 9950 ⓦ www.cherryjam.net ⓛ 18.00–02.00 Mon–Sat, 16.00–24.00 Sun ⓝ Royal Oak

Notting Hill Arts Club The scene changes nightly from live bands to DJs to assorted happenings at this funky, creative basement club. ⓐ 21 Notting Hill Gate ⓣ 020 7460 4459 ⓦ www.nottinghillartsclub.com ⓛ 18.00–02.00 Mon–Fri, 16.00–02.00 Sat, 16.00–01.00 Sun ⓝ Notting Hill Gate

606 Club Musicians hang out at this hip Chelsea jazz club, with live music nightly by British artists. It's also a restaurant, and alcohol is only served with meals. ⓐ 90 Lots Road ⓣ 020 7352 5953 ⓦ www.606club.co.uk ⓛ 19.30–01.30 Mon–Wed, 20.00–01.30 Thur, 20.00–02.00 Fri & Sat, 20.00–24.00 Sun ⓝ Fulham Broadway

The City & East End

London's financial district is simply known as The City, or the Square Mile. This was the birthplace of the capital, and the district today is only slightly larger than the old Roman walls that once enclosed it. Two of London's greatest landmarks still stand, and after you've seen St Paul's and the Tower, head further into the East End for a taste of the old London. Several of London's most famous markets are located here. Both areas are easily walkable, and served by several Tube stations and bus routes.

SIGHTS & ATTRACTIONS

Brick Lane
It's synonymous with a market, curry houses and a best-selling novel, and now this narrow East End street is a byword for London's latest 'hot' area. The road was named for the brick kilns that operated here in the 17th century. For the past 40 years or so it's been the centre of the local Bengali community, so much so that the borough named the southern half 'Bangla Town'. The hip part of Brick Lane is further north around the Old Truman Brewery, which has been redeveloped as a music, art and design centre with trendy cafés, bars and fashion shops nearby. ⊙ Liverpool Street, Aldgate East

The Monument
Topped with a copper flame, this fluted column designed by Sir Christopher Wren commemorates the Great Fire of London in 1666. It stands 62 m (203 ft) high, the exact distance to the start of the fire at a bakery in Pudding Lane. You can climb the 311 spiral steps to the top to the viewing platform.

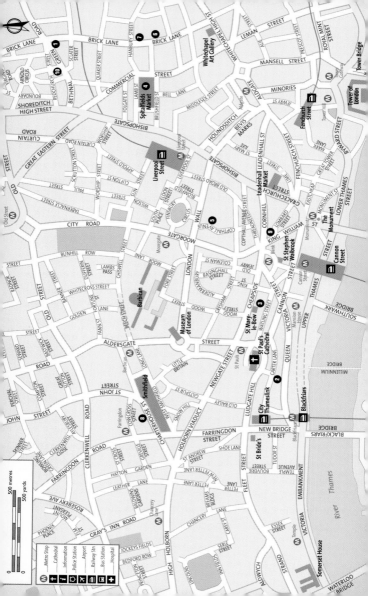

THE CITY

ⓐ Monument Street ☎ 020 7626 2717 ⓦ www.cityoflondon.gov.uk
🕐 10.00–17.30; admission charge Ⓜ Monument

Spitalfields

One of the city's most fascinating areas, Spitalfields was the heart of
the old East End. The focal point of the area is the covered Old
Spitalfields Market, though its recent redevelopment is a sure sign
that gentrification of the area is setting in. It still retains part of its
original façade on Brushfield Street, and some of the old fruit-and-
veg shop signs. Ⓜ Liverpool Street

St Paul's Cathedral

The magnificent dome of St Paul's – 111 m (364 ft) high and the
second-largest in the world after St Peter's in Rome – has made it a
London landmark. It was designed by Sir Christopher Wren to
replace the medieval cathedral destroyed in the Great Fire, and took
35 years to build. There is much to admire in the splendid baroque
interior, from the frescoes on the dome to the massive arches,
ironwork screens and carved choir stalls.
ⓐ Ludgate Hill ☎ 020 7236 4128 ⓦ www.stpauls.co.uk
🕐 08.30–16.00 Mon–Sat; admission charge Ⓜ St Paul's

Tower Bridge

London's most ornate bridge, completed in 1894, features neo-
Gothic towers of granite and Portland stone, but they cover a core
of steel. This enables the centre section to be raised, allowing tall
ships to pass. Try and time your visit to see this amazing sight
(☎ 020 7940 3984 to find out the schedule).
ⓐ Tower Bridge ☎ 020 7403 3761 ⓦ www.towerbridge.org.uk
🕐 09.30–18.00; admission charge Ⓜ Tower Hill

Tower of London

The walls of this massive fortress hold nearly 1,000 years of British history. From William the Conqueror's White Tower, subsequent monarchs expanded the defences with walls, a moat and more buildings to create the 7.3-hectare World Heritage Site that stands today. The Yeoman Warders, or 'Beefeaters', wearing Tudor uniforms relay much of its history on entertaining tours. For many the highlight is the Jewel House, which displays the Crown Jewels.
ⓐ Tower Hill ⓣ 020 7709 0765 ⓦ www.hrp.org.uk ⓛ 09.00–18.00 Tues–Sat, 10.00–18.00 Sun & Mon, Mar–Oct; closes 17.00 Nov–Feb; admission charge ⓜ Tower Hill

CULTURE

Museum of London

London's long history from prehistoric times to the 20th century is portrayed in appealing displays spread over two floors. Among the highlights are an eerie audio-visual that portrays London burning

WREN'S CHURCHES

Apart from his masterpiece St Paul's, Sir Christopher Wren designed 51 churches in the City after the Great Fire. More than half of them still stand today. St Stephen Walbrook (39 Walbrook) is considered to be his finest and is the Lord Mayor's official church. It's said that a true Cockney must be born within the sound of the bells of St Mary-le-Bow in Cheapside. Lovely St Bride's off Fleet Street with its tiered steeple was the inspiration for the traditional shape of wedding cakes.

during the Great Fire, life-size models of Victorian streets and shops, and the opulent gilded Lord Mayor's Coach.

ⓐ London Wall ⓣ 0870 444 3852 ⓦ www.museumoflondon.org.uk
ⓛ 10.00–17.50 Mon–Sat, 12.00–17.50 Sun ⓝ Barbican, St Paul's

Whitechapel Art Gallery

Built in 1901 with the aim of bringing art to the people of the East End, the gallery stages some of London's most novel contemporary art exhibitions featuring major and emerging artists.

ⓐ Whitechapel High Street ⓣ 020 7522 7888
ⓦ www.whitechapel.org ⓛ 11.00–18.00 Tues–Sun, until 21.00 Thur
ⓝ Aldgate East

RETAIL THERAPY

Shopping Streets & Markets

Brick Lane Market Loads of second-hand gear, from clothes to you-name-it spills out along Brick Lane and its side streets north of the railway bridge. You could browse for hours, and you just might find a bargain. ⓐ Brick Lane ⓛ 08.00–14.00 ⓝ Aldgate East, Shoreditch

Columbia Road Flower Market This small street becomes a riot of colour on Sundays when it's lined with plants and cut flowers. Many interesting design shops have sprung up in the area. ⓐ Columbia Road ⓛ 07.00–14.00 Sun ⓝ Shoreditch

Leadenhall Market With its beautifully ornate iron and glass roof and stone arches, this Victorian market hall is an attraction in itself.

◗ *The landmark Tower Bridge acts as a gateway in from the east*

There has been a produce market here since Roman times, but these days it's filled with shops and pubs, and the market stalls selling cheese, wine, fish, poultry, meat and chocolates cater mainly for City workers on their lunch breaks. 🅐 Whittington Avenue 🕐 07.00–16.00 Mon–Fri 🅝 Monument, Bank

Petticoat Lane Nick-named for the undergarments sold here in the 18th century, this is a big, bustling East End market with Cockney stall-holders hawking clothes, accessories, household wares and bric-a-brac. Look carefully and you can find some fashion bargains, particularly leather jackets and fabrics. Sunday (🕐 09.00–15.00) is the main day, some stalls also operate 🕐 10.00–15.00 Mon–Fri. 🅐 Middlesex Street 🅝 Liverpool Street

Spitalfields Market The character of this historic Victorian market still shines through, despite controversial renovations. It's a great place for creative crafts, jewellery, accessories, gifts, music, trendy fashions by young designers, and organic foods. 🅐 Brushfield Street 🕐 10.00–16.00 Mon–Fri & Sun (general); organic food stalls 10.00–16.00 Wed & Sun; fashion 10.30–16.00 Fri 🅝 Liverpool Street, Aldgate East

TAKING A BREAK

Brick Lane Beigel Bake £ ❶ The tasty fillings, cheap prices and 24-hour service have made this busy takeaway shop an East End institution. 🅐 159 Brick Lane ☎ 020 7729 0616 🕐 24 hours 🅝 Shoreditch

De Gustibus £ ❷   English breakfasts, sandwiches, soups and a fantastic salad bar are all complemented by the delicious breads from this artisan bakery. ⓐ 53–55 Carter Lane ❶ 020 7236 0056 ⓦ www.degustibus.co.uk ❶ 07.00–17.00 Mon–Fri Ⓜ St Paul's

The Place Below £ ❸   A creative vegetarian restaurant is tucked away in the crypt of the Church of St Mary-le-Bow. ⓐ Cheapside ❶ 020 7329 0789 ❶ 07.30–15.30 Mon–Fri Ⓜ St Paul's, Bank

Arkansas Café £–££ ❹   Ribs, burgers and beef brisket get smoked the southern USA way, with the chef's special homemade barbecue sauce. ⓐ Unit 12, Old Spitalfields Market ❶ 020 7377 6999 ❶ 12.00–14.30 Mon–Fri, 12.00–16.00 Sun Ⓜ Liverpool Street

K10 £–££ ❺   Upstairs this sushi restaurant runs a busy takeaway, downstairs it's a kaiten, or conveyor belt, affair where you choose your dishes as they pass by. ⓐ 20 Copthall Avenue ❶ 020 7562 8510 ⓦ www.k10.net ❶ 11.30–15.00 Mon–Fri, takeaway until 18.00 Ⓜ Moorgate

AFTER DARK

Restaurants

Café Naz £–££ ❻   The modern dishes and decor are a welcome addition to the Brick Lane curry house scene. The service gets mixed reviews, but most people like the Indian and Bangladeshi cuisine, cooked in both traditional and contemporary ways. ⓐ 46–48 Brick Lane ❶ 020 7247 0234 ❶ 12.00–24.00 Mon–Wed, 12.00–01.00 Thur–Fri, 18.00–01.00 Sat, 12.00–15.00, 18.00–24.00 Sun Ⓜ Aldgate East, Shoreditch

The Monsoon £–££ ❼ Diners rave about the food at this welcoming curry house, and Brick Lane regulars rate it a cut above the rest. Contemporary decor, low prices and good service to match. ⓐ 78 Brick Lane ☎ 020 7375 1345 🕐 12.00–24.00 or 01.00 Ⓜ Aldgate East, Shoreditch

Smith's of Smithfield ££ ❽ Located in an old warehouse next to the Smithfield Meat Market, the restaurant serves modern British cuisine made from organic produce. There are wonderful views of the City and St Paul's from the upper floors. There's also a bar and café on the ground floor. ⓐ 67–77 Charterhouse Street ☎ 020 7251 7950 Ⓦ www.smithsofsmithfield.co.uk 🕐 12.00–15.00, 18.00–23.00 Mon–Fri, 18.00–22.45 Sat Ⓜ Farringdon

1 Lombard Street ££–£££ ❾ The contemporary European cuisine is as stylish as the decor at this City brasserie, which is humming and hopping with activity round its circular bar, set beneath a beautiful glass dome. ⓐ 1 Lombard Street ☎ 020 7929 6611 Ⓦ www.1lombardstreet.com 🕐 12.00–15.00, 18.00–22.00 Mon–Fri Ⓜ Bank

Les Trois Garcons £££ ❿ The madly camp decor in this unique converted pub lightens up the seriously good cooking. Amidst the stuffed animals, glitzy handbags, etched mirrors and chandeliers, you'll dine on creative French dishes and lovely seafood. ⓐ 1 Club Row ☎ 020 7613 1924 Ⓦ www.lestroisgarcons.com 🕐 19.00–22.30 Mon–Thur, 18.45–23.00 Fri–Sat Ⓜ Shoreditch

---

▶ *Canada Tower stands tall among the skyscrapers of the Docklands*

Cinemas & Theatres
The Barbican Within this huge concrete complex of flats lies an arts centre, and it's worth making your way through the maze for the changing exhibitions at its two art galleries or its programme of performing arts. The Barbican is home to the London Symphony Orchestra, and concerts of classical, jazz and world music are also staged here. Theatre performances take place in the Barbican Theatre and the Pit, while the two cinemas show art-house and independent films. ❸ Silk Street ❶ 020 7638 8891 ❸ 09.00–20.00 Mon–Sun ❷ Barbican

Bars, Clubs & Discos
Black Friar Stained glass, mosaics and art nouveau carvings make this century-old pub one of the loveliest in the City. A glass of ale (a good range to choose from) and a pie (their speciality) don't come any better. ❸ 174 Queen Victoria Street ❶ 020 7236 5474 ❸ 11.00–23.00 Mon–Wed & Sat, 11.00–23.30 Thur–Fri, 12.00–22.30 Sun ❷ Blackfriars

Cargo Set in an old railway arch, this cool, upmarket bar-restaurant-club has first-rate club nights that often feature live bands. ❸ 83 Rivington Street ❶ 020 7739 3440 ❿ www.cargo-london.com ❸ 11.00–01.00 Mon–Thur, 11.00–03.00 Fri, 18.00–03.00 Sat, 13.00–24.00 Sun ❷ Old Street

Plastic People With a superb sound system and music that ranges from rock to hip-hop, jazz to Latin, this Shoreditch club is bliss for music lovers, despite the crowded dance floor. ❸ 147–149 Curtain Road ❶ 020 7739 6471 ❿ www.plasticpeople.co.uk ❸ 22.00–02.00 Mon–Thur, 22.00–03.30 Fri & Sat, 19.30–24.00 Sun ❷ Old Street

Vertigo 42 The view from the 42nd-floor champagne bar of the City's tallest building is incredible, and worth the pricy drinks and bar menu. Advance booking is essential. ⓐ Tower 42, 25 Old Broad Street ⓣ 020 7877 7842 ⓦ www.vertigo42.co.uk ⓛ 12.00–15.00, 17.00–23.00 Mon–Fri ⓝ Bank, Liverpool Street

Vibe Bar The Old Truman Brewery is the hub of Brick Lane's trendy set, especially at its popular watering hole with alternating DJs and live bands, and a great courtyard beer garden in summer. ⓐ 91–95 Brick Lane ⓣ 020 7426 0491 ⓦ www.vibe-bar.co.uk ⓛ 11.00–23.30 Mon–Thur & Sun, 11.00–01.00 Fri & Sat ⓝ Aldgate East, Liverpool Street

Ye Olde Cheshire Cheese A maze of atmospheric rooms with fireplaces, wooden benches and bare floorboards make up this historic 18th-century pub frequented by London's literary lights. Entrance from Wine Office Court. ⓐ 145 Fleet Street ⓣ 020 7353 6170 ⓦ www.yeoldecheshirecheese.com ⓛ 11.00–23.00 Mon–Sat, 12.00–14.30 Sun ⓝ Blackfriars

⬤ *The perfect haunt for discovering the key to some English classics*

South of the river

In Shakespeare's day the south side of the Thames was the place for theatre and entertainment. Today the South Bank is still a centre for the arts, with a world-class art gallery, the South Bank Centre performing arts complex, and the reconstructed Globe Theatre. Tube stations are more widely spaced here, and the best way to reach many attractions is across a bridge from the north bank, so put on your walking shoes.

SIGHTS & ATTRACTIONS

HMS *Belfast*

The last of the great armoured warships from the first half of the 20th century is permanently moored on the Thames, upstream from Tower Bridge. A tour of its nine decks takes in the operations deck, gun turrets, officers' cabins, galley, sickbay, boiler and engine rooms, with life-size models and re-enactments of battles and life at sea.

ⓐ Morgan's Lane, Tooley Street ⓣ 020 7940 6300
ⓦ www.iwm.org.uk/belfast ⓛ 10.00–18.00 Mar–Oct, until 17.00 Nov–Feb; admission charge ⓝ London Bridge

London Aquarium

One of Europe's largest aquariums is submerged beneath County Hall. It contains a shark and stingray tank three floors high, scores of colourful tropical fish and a petting tank full of manta rays.

ⓐ County Hall, Westminster Bridge Road ⓣ 020 7967 8000
ⓦ www.londonaquarium.co.uk ⓛ 10.00–18.00; admission charge
ⓝ Waterloo, Westminster

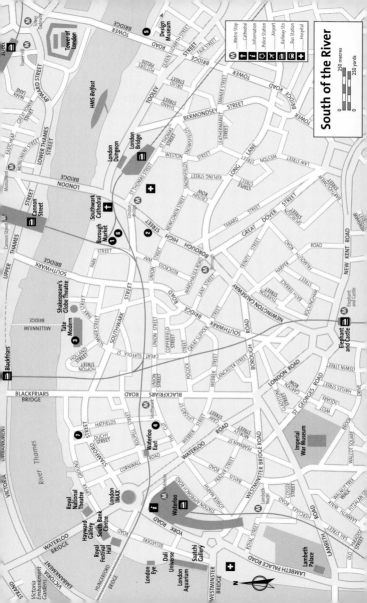

South of the River

Legend:
- Ⓜ Metro Stop
- ✝ Cathedral
- ℹ Information
- 🔶 Police Station
- ✈ Airport
- 🚉 Railway Stn
- 🚌 Bus Station
- ✚ Hospital

0   250 metres
0   250 yards

Map labels:

Tower Bridge
Tower of London
Tower Hill
Tower Subway
Design Museum ⑤
Tooley Street
HMS Belfast
Queen Elizabeth Street
Potters Fields
Shad Thames Street
Gainsford Street
Fair Street
Tower Bridge Road
Duke Street Hill
Bermondsey Street
Leathermarket Street
Tanner Street
Long Lane
Weston Street
Kipling Street
Snowsfields
Crosby Row
Staple Street
Law Street
St Thomas Street
London Dungeon
London Bridge
Southwark Cathedral ✝
Borough Market ①⑥
Tabard Street
Great Dover Street
New Kent Road
Trinity Street
Pilgrimage Street
Harper Road
Falmouth Road
Swan Street
Marshalsea Road
Lant Street
Redcross Way
Borough High Street
Newcomen Street
Borough ②
Mint Street
Pocock Street
Webber Street
Lancaster Street
Great Suffolk Street
Copperfield Street
Union Street
Sumner Street
Hopton Street
Holland Street
Tate Modern ③
Shakespeare's Globe Theatre
Park Street
Clink Street
Bankside
Millennium Bridge
Blackfriars 🚉
Upper Ground
Southwark Bridge
Cannon Street 🚉
Blackfriars Bridge
Blackfriars Road
Southwark Street
Newington Causeway
Bath Terrace
Rockingham Street
Elephant and Castle Ⓜ
London Road
St Georges Road
Gladstone Street
Garden Row
Brook Drive
Hayles Street
West Square
Oswin Street
Imperial War Museum
Webber Street
Gray Street
Ufford Street
Cornwall Road
Hatfields
Duchy Street
Roupell Street
Theed Street
Waterloo East 🚉 ④
Stamford Street
The Cut
Waterloo Road
Royal National Theatre
London IMAX
South Bank Centre
Hayward Gallery
Royal Festival Hall
Hungerford Bridge
Waterloo ℹ ② Ⓜ
York Road
Station Approach Road
Baylis Road
Waterloo Road
Westminster Bridge Road
Kennington Road
Lambeth North Ⓜ
Hercules Road
Cosser Street
Walcot Square
Brook Drive
Sail Street
Walnut Tree Walk
Fitzalan Street
Lambeth Walk
Old Paradise Street
Lambeth Road
Lambeth Palace Road
Lambeth Palace
Saatchi Gallery
Dali Universe
London Eye
London Aquarium
Westminster Bridge
Victoria Embankment Gardens
Victoria Embankment
Waterloo Bridge
Strand
River Thames
Belvedere Road
Upper Ground
Addington Street

N

London Dungeon

The gruesome exhibits at this museum in the vaults under London Bridge rail station are not for the squeamish. The Gothic horrors presented here, through waxwork tableaux, costumed actors and re-enactments of grisly scenes from London's history, include Jack the Ripper, the Great Fire and the Great Plague.

📍 Tooley Street 📞 020 7403 7221 🌐 www.thedungeons.com
🕐 10.00–19.30 mid-July–early Sept, 10.00–17.30 rest of the year; admission charge Ⓝ London Bridge

London Eye

It's the largest observation wheel in the world and one of the best experiences in London. Transparent pods slowly revolve to a height of 135 m (443 ft) above the city, giving you spectacular panoramic views over the city in all directions. This birds-eye view shows off London's landmarks in a new light.

📍 County Hall, Westminster Bridge Road 📞 0870 5000 600
🌐 www.ba-londoneye.com 🕐 09.30–20.00 Feb–Apr and Oct–Dec, 09.30–21.00 May–Jun & Sept, 09.30–22.00 July–Aug, closed Jan–early Feb for annual maintenance; admission charge
Ⓝ Waterloo, Westminster ❶ The ride takes 30 minutes but the queues can be much longer than that in high season. You can book a timed ticket in advance, but there's no guarantee on the weather

Millennium Bridge

When it was erected in 2000, this Millennium milestone was the first pedestrian bridge to be built across the Thames in more than 100 years. It connects two of London's great sights: St Paul's Cathedral in the City and the Tate Modern art gallery (also opened in the Millennium year) on the South Bank. The 325-m (1,066-ft) high steel bridge was designed by architect Norman Foster and engineer Ove Arup.

Southwark Cathedral

Over 700 years old, Southwark Cathedral was built as a medieval priory church. Though much of the interior was rebuilt in Victorian times, it retained its choir and lovely stone Tudor screen, which are among the oldest Gothic architecture in London.

ⓐ Cathedral Street ⓣ 020 7367 6700
ⓦ www.dswark.org/cathedral ⓛ 08.00–18.00 Mon–Fri, 09.00–17.00 Sat, 12.30–17.00 Sun ⓝ London Bridge

CULTURE

Dalí Universe

Although Salvadore Dalí's greatest Surrealist works are elsewhere, his popularity is such that this museum dedicated to his art is a big hit with visitors. Top attractions include a copy of his Mae West Lips sofa and his painting from Hitchcock's movie *Spellbound*.

ⓐ County Hall, South Bank ⓣ 020 7620 2720
ⓦ www.daliuniverse.com ⓛ 10.00–17.30 (last entry); admission charge ⓝ Westminster, Waterloo

Design Museum

Set in a converted warehouse on Butlers Wharf, this showcase for 20th- and 21st-century design was conceived by Sir Terence Conran, creator of Habitat. It focuses on everyday objects in a series of changing exhibits that highlight innovative ideas, products, designers and technologies.

ⓐ 28 Shad Thames, Butlers Wharf ⓣ 0870 833 9955

Ⓦ www.designmuseum.org Ⓛ 10.00–17.45, until 21.00 Fri; admission charge Ⓝ London Bridge, Tower Bridge

Imperial War Museum

A huge array of military weapons and vehicles, from a V2 rocket to a Spitfire, is on display at this museum examining wars of Britain or the Commonwealth, from World War I to the present.
Ⓐ Lambeth Road Ⓣ 020 7416 5320 Ⓦ www.iwm.org.uk
Ⓛ 10.00–18.00 Ⓝ Lambeth North, Elephant and Castle

Saatchi Gallery

Art collector Charles Saatchi's private collection of contemporary art is displayed in the former council chamber of the County Hall building. Its changing exhibitions often feature works by the so-called Young British Artists (of whom Damien Hirst and Tracey Emin are most famous) who Saatchi helped to promote.
Ⓐ County Hall, South Bank Ⓣ 020 7928 8195
Ⓦ www.saatchi-gallery.co.uk Ⓛ 10.00–20.00 Sun–Thur, 10.00–22.00 Fri & Sat; admission charge Ⓝ Waterloo

Shakespeare's Globe Theatre

Performances of this reconstructed Shakespearian theatre take place in natural daylight, as they did in the Bard's day. For a fiver you can stand in the pitt as the groundlings once did, or opt for seats (and cushions) in the stalls. Below in the UnderGlobe is a fascinating exhibition that tells you all about the theatre in Shakespeare's day, with insights into the Bard's life and times.
Ⓐ 21 New Globe Walk Ⓣ 020 7902 1400 Ⓦ www.shakespeares-globe.org Ⓛ 10.00–17.00, theatre tours mornings only May–Sept; admission charge Ⓝ Blackfriars, London Bridge, Mansion House

South Bank Centre

London's largest arts centre sprawls along the South Bank. Its riverside promenade makes a lively place on a fine day with strollers, skaters, buskers, and browsers at the weekend book stalls here. The Royal Festival Hall, its most accessible building, is the home of the London Philharmonic. Interesting exhibitions and events are held in the large foyer, and it's worth wandering in to see what's going on. Other performing venues include the Queen Elizabeth Hall, the Purcell Room, the Royal National Theatre and the National Film Theatre. The Hayward Gallery hosts blockbuster art exhibitions, often focusing on contemporary British artists.

⬤ *Reconstruction of the theatre where Shakespeare's plays were first performed*

☎ 020 7921 0600 general information, 020 7960 5226 Hayward Gallery ⓦ www.sbc.org.uk or www.hayward.org.uk 🕐 Foyer 10.00–22.30, Hayward Gallery 10.00–18.00, until 20.00 Tues & Wed Ⓜ Waterloo, Embankment

Tate Modern
From 1995 to 2000, the disused Bankside power station was transformed into the stellar attraction of London's art world. Tate Modern is one of the largest and finest modern art museums in the world, focusing on art from 1900 to the present day. Paintings are rotated regularly, but works by the great 20th-century artists, including Matisse, Picasso, Dalí, Warhol and Rothko, are always on show.
Ⓐ Bankside ☎ 020 7887 8000 ⓦ www.tate.org.uk 🕐 10.00–18.00 Sun–Thur, until 22.00 Fri & Sat Ⓜ London Bridge, Blackfriars

RETAIL THERAPY

Shopping Streets & Markets
Borough Market Set under Victorian railway arches, this is the most atmospheric and arguably the best food market in London. During the week and early morning hours it operates as a wholesale produce market, as it has done since the mid-18th century. But Thursday to Saturday it opens its doors to thousands of food lovers, who come for the stalls selling organic meats and veg, poultry, game, cheeses, seafood, coffee, tea, sweets and foodstuffs from Spain, Italy and more. Ⓐ 8 Southwark Street ☎ 020 7407 1002 ⓦ www.boroughmarket.org.uk 🕐 10.00–17.00 Thur, 12.00–18.00 Fri, 09.00–16.00 Sat Ⓜ London Bridge

Design Museum For a fashionable and unusual gift, check out the selection at this museum shop, with items by well-known names – and new designers who soon will be. ⓐ 28 Shad Thames, Butlers Wharf ⓣ 0870 833 9955 ⓦ www.designmuseum.org ⓛ 10.00–17.45 Mon–Sun ⓝ London Bridge, Tower Bridge, DLR: ShadThames

Gabriel's Wharf You can find some unique jewellery, clothing, textiles, ceramics, glassware and other furnishings in the craft and design shops here, part of a community redevelopment of this riverside site damaged by World War II bombs. ⓐ 56 Upper Ground ⓦ www.gabrielswharf.co.uk ⓛ 09.30–18.00 Fri–Sun ⓝ Waterloo

Hays Galleria This attractive complex was one of the first redevelopments of the old docklands, with shops and restaurants lining a courtyard covered by a glass atrium. ⓐ Tooley Street ⓝ London Bridge

TAKING A BREAK

Konditor & Cook £ ❶ There are three Southside locations for this top-notch bakery and sandwich shop: behind Borough Market, another near Waterloo station and one in the Design Museum. The soups, salads, cakes and desserts are irresistible. ⓐ 10 Stoney Street, Borough Market; ⓣ 020 7407 5100; 020 7261 0456 ⓦ www.konditorandcook.com ⓛ 07.30–18.00 Mon–Fri, 08.30–16.00 Sat ⓝ London Bridge, Southwark, Waterloo

Tas Café £ ❷ Two doors down from its big sister restaurant, this delightful Turkish café has a handful of tables and a takeaway counter with a great choice of salads, falafel, soups, coffee and pastries. 76 Borough High Street 020 7403 8557 12.00–23.30 Mon–Sat, until 22.30 Sun London Bridge

Tate Modern Café £–££ The museum café on Level 2 serves breakfast, lunch and tea with a menu of good British fare. Tapas is also served on late opening nights. Tate Modern, Bankside 020 7401 5014 www.tate.org.uk 10.00–17.30 Mon–Thur & Sun, 10.00–21.30 Fri & Sat London Bridge, Blackfriars

AFTER DARK

Restaurants
Anchor & Hope ££ Excellent modern British cooking in a friendly, laid-back atmosphere has earned this South Bank gastropub a great reputation. There's good beer, too, and a long wine list. 36 The Cut 020 7928 9898 17.00–23.00 Mon, 11.00–23.00 Tues–Sat Waterloo, Southwark

Butlers Wharf Chop House ££–£££ Part of the Conran stable, this spacious Thames-side restaurant is the place for lovers of traditional English food. In summer, tables on the long terrace offer great views of Tower Bridge. Butlers Wharf Building, 36e Shad Thames 020 7403 3403 www.conran-restaurants.co.uk 12.00–15.00 Mon–Sun, 18.00–23.00 Mon–Sat Tower Hill, London Bridge

Roast ££–£££ 'Deliciously British' describes the philosophy and cuisine of this sleek restaurant, set in the renovated Floral Hall in the arches of Borough Market. The impressive menu features the finest seasonal produce sourced around the country. The set menus are very good value and there's a tasting menu, too. ⓐ Floral Hall, Stoney Street ⓣ 020 7940 1300 ⓦ www.roast-restaurant.com ⓛ 07.00–10.00, 12.00–15.00, 17.30–23.00 Mon–Fri, 08.00–11.00, 11.30–16.00, 18.00–23.00 Sat, 09.00–11.30, 12.00–16.00 Sun ⓝ London Bridge

Oxo Tower £££ ❼ The menu is pricy but the views over the Thames are out of this world. Dine in the retro-style Brasserie and try to get a seat on the balcony in summer. The more formal restaurant features modern British cuisine and glorious floor-to-ceiling windows for a romantic night-time view. ⓐ Oxo Tower Wharf ⓣ 020 7803 3888 ⓛ 12.00–15.00, 18.00–23.30 ⓝ Blackfriars

Cinemas & Theatres
National Film Theatre The capital's finest cinema programmes are offered here, ranging from the best of British and international films to retrospectives. It's also the hub of the London Film Festival each year. ⓐ South Bank complex ⓣ 020 7928 3232 ⓦ www.bfi.org.uk/nft ⓝ Embankment, Waterloo

Old Vic Hollywood star Kevin Spacey is now the artistic director of this venerable playhouse where Britain's National Theatre has its roots.
ⓐ The Cut, Waterloo Road
ⓣ 0870 060 6628
ⓦ www.oldvictheatre.com
ⓝ Waterloo

🔺 *There's more to the South Bank than art*

Royal Festival Hall One of London's major venues for classical concerts and dance productions, the Royal Festival Hall is due to reopen in early 2007 after a major refurbishment. ⓐ South Bank Centre ⓘ 020 7960 4242 ⓦ www.sbc.org.uk Ⓜ Waterloo

Bars, Clubs & Discos
Anchor Bankside One of the best places in London for outdoor drinking besides the Thames, the interior rooms of this historic pub still have many of their original 18th-century features such as wood beams and dark-wood panelling. ⓐ 34 Park Street ⓘ 020 7407 1577 ⓛ 11.00–23.00 Mon–Sat, 12.00–22.30 Sun Ⓜ London Bridge

George Inn A side alley leads to the large cobbled courtyard of this 17th-century coaching inn, the only galleried inn of its type left in the city. Inside are the connecting rooms and bars of a traditional tavern, while the courtyard is a lively place on fine evenings and at lunchtime. Real ales and good bar food are served. ⓐ 77 Borough High Street ⓘ 020 7407 2056 ⓛ 11.00–23.00 Mon–Sat, 12.00–22.30 Sun Ⓜ London Bridge

Ministry of Sound One of the biggest names in clubbing, this famous club has its huge home base in Southwark, where it packs in the punters with its state of the art sound system and top-name DJs from home and abroad. Queues are long and prices are high. ⓐ 103 Gaunt Street ⓘ 020 7378 6528 ⓦ www.ministryofsound.co.uk ⓛ 22.00–03.00 Wed, 22.30–05.00 Fri, 23.00–07.00 Sat Ⓜ Elephant and Castle

---

▶ *Head to Camden Lock if you'd like to ride on a canal boat*

OUT OF TOWN
trips

Beyond the City Centre

Several of London's most interesting places and attractions lie beyond the city centre but are still within the greater metropolitan area. These include good museums, botanical gardens, parks and open spaces, and one of Britain's finest royal palaces. All of the sights and attractions mentioned here are easily reached by tube, bus or rail in under an hour, and if you decide to stay and check out the nightlife, a taxi back to your hotel won't break the bank.

SIGHTS & ATTRACTIONS

Camden Town
There's still a hard-edged hipness to Camden Town, despite efforts over the past 20 years to regenerate its rougher edges. The main reason to come here is for the funky shops and sprawling weekend market (see p134) which has become a tourist attraction, especially with young visitors looking for offbeat fashions and clubwear. Camden also has a thriving nightlife and music scene – MTV studios are based here in the former TV-AM building, a striking modern landmark along the canal on Hawley Crescent. At Camden Lock, you can take a canal boat ride along Regent's Canal, past Regent's Park to Little Venice.
ⓐ Camden Waterbus, Camden Lock ❶ 020 7482 2660 ◐ daily Apr–Sept, reduced hours in winter Ⓝ Camden Town

Cutty Sark
You can board the fastest of the old tea clippers, which broke the record for sailing between London and China in just 107 days. Built in 1869, it is the last of its kind and is moored alongside Greenwich Pier.

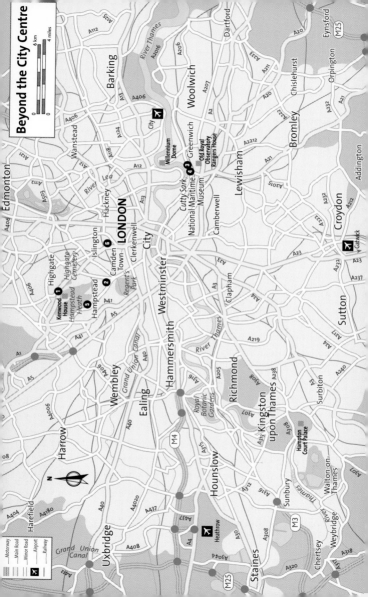

Beyond the City Centre

0 km 6
0 4 miles

N

Motorway
Main Road
Minor Road
Airport
Railway

Harefield
Uxbridge
Harrow
Wembley
Ealing
Hammersmith
Hounslow
Heathrow
Staines
Kingston upon Thames
Hampton Court Palace
Richmond
Royal Botanic Gardens
Sunbury
Walton-on-Thames
Weybridge
Chertsey
Sutton
Croydon
Addington
Bromley
Chislehurst
Orpington
Eynsford
Dartford
Woolwich
Greenwich
Old Royal Observatory
Ranger's House
National Maritime Museum
Cutty Sark
Millennium Dome
Lewisham
Camberwell
Clapham
Westminster
City
LONDON
Clerkenwell
Islington
Camden Town
Regent's Park
Hackney
Hampstead
Hampstead Heath
Highgate
Highgate Cemetery
Kenwood House
Wanstead
Barking
Edmonton

Grand Union Canal

River Thames
River Lea
River Brent

1 Kenwood House
5 Hampstead
2 Camden Town
6 Islington
3 Old Royal Observatory
4 Greenwich

📞 020 8858 3445 🌐 www.cuttysark.org.uk 🕐 10.00–17.00; admission charge Ⓜ DLR Cutty Sark

Greenwich

Downriver from central London on the south side of the Thames, Greenwich is an attractive place to visit for its weekend market, and to see the historic buildings and attractions in and around Greenwich Park. Its architectural highlight is the Old Royal Naval College, which replaced the Tudor palace which once stood here along the river. Greenwich also has good riverside paths and pubs. You can even walk the 2.4 km (1½ miles) downstream to the *Millennium Dome*, which, with its 49-m (160-ft) height and 0.8 km (½ mile)-plus circumference, is the largest dome in the world. It is being renovated as a music and sports arena, due to open in 2007. You'll get the best views of Greenwich if you come by riverboat from Westminster Pier or Tower Bridge (see page 82). Or take the Docklands Light Railway to Island Gardens for the view of the Royal Naval College across the Thames, then take the foot tunnel under the river. You can also come by DLR to Cutty Sark, or by train to Greenwich station. Greenwich Gateway Visitor Center.

📍 Pepys Building beside the Cutty Sark 📞 0870 608 2000
🕐 10.00–17.00

Hampstead & the Heath

With its winding lanes and Georgian town houses, Hampstead village retains its historic charms. Over two centuries it has been home to many writers and artists, from John Keats to John le Carré. There are several historic houses to visit, but it's also fun just to stroll its atmospheric streets and alleyways, or while away a few hours in the fashionable shops and cafés along High Street or Flask

Walk. Adjoining the village is Hampstead Heath, a vast open space of some 324 hectares (800 acres) that is wonderful for long walks. It feels quite wild in places, with its rolling grassland, thick woodland and natural ponds, some of which are used for bathing. There are wonderful views over London from Parliament Hill.

Hampton Court Palace

Of all Britain's royal palaces, this one on the banks of the Thames is the finest and most enjoyable to visit. From its Tudor chimneys to its sweeping formal gardens, it's highly atmospheric. Join the regular tours by costumed guides for an entertaining insight into palace life

🔺 *Greenwich is home to the Old Royal Naval College*

through the ages. You could easily spend a full day here to take everything in, especially if you want to stroll in the gardens and try your luck in the Maze. In summer, the riverboat from Westminster (see page 82) makes a grand arrival.

ⓐ East Molesey, Surrey ❶ 0870 752 7777 Ⓦ www.hrp.org.uk
🕐 10.00–18.00 Apr–Oct, 10.00–16.30 Nov–Mar; admission charge
Ⓝ British Rail to Hampton Court

Highgate Cemetery

Highgate, another historic village, borders Hampstead Heath on the eastern side. Its main attraction is the Victorian Highgate Cemetery, divided into two parts, where illustrious figures from London's history lie. The Gothic West Cemetery, overgrown and creepily atmospheric, inspired Bram Stoker's *Dracula*.

❶ 020 8340 1834 Ⓦ www.highgate-cemetery.org ❶ Admission charge Ⓝ Highgate, Archway

Islington & Clerkenwell

The area around Islington's Upper Street and parts of Clerkenwell, the area that lies between it and the City, are two of the most prominent gentrified areas of North London. The many good bars, restaurants and lively nightlife are their biggest attraction, and there's good shopping along Upper Street and nearby markets. Islington also has several highly regarded theatres, while Clerkenwell has become a hot area for nightclubs.

Ⓝ Highbury & Islington, Angel

Old Royal Observatory

Set in a building designed by Sir Christopher Wren for the first Astronomer Royal, John Flamsteed, the observatory was founded in

1675 by Charles II. Now filled with early telescopes and other instruments, as well as a modern astronomy gallery and camera obscura, it's one of Britain's most fascinating museums.
ⓐ Greenwich Park ❶ 020 8312 6565 ⓦ www.rog.nmm.ac.uk
🕓 10.00–17.00, until 18.00 July–Aug Ⓝ DLR Cutty Sark

Regent's Park

This royal park was designed by John Nash, whose elegant neoclassical terraces ring the east side along the Outer Circle. In addition to its pleasant green space, the park's attractions include Queen Mary's Garden with its beautiful roses, an open-air theatre that stages Shakespeare plays in summer, a boating lake and the London Zoo (see pages 149–150) ❶ 020 7486 7905
ⓦ www.royalparks.gov.uk Ⓝ Baker Street, Regent's Park

Royal Botanic Gardens

Better known simply as Kew Gardens, this beautiful park landscaped by Capability Brown has been a botanical research centre since the 1770s. Highlights include the Palm House, the Temperate House and the Princess of Wales Conservatory with its giant water lilies.
ⓐ Kew, Richmond, Surrey ❶ 020 8332 5655 ⓦ www.kew.org
🕓 09.30–18.30 Mon–Fri, until 19.30 weekends late Mar–Aug, 09.30–18.00 Sept–Oct, 09.30–16.15 Nov–early Feb, 09.30–17.30 early Feb–late Mar; admission charge Ⓝ Kew Gardens

CULTURE

Kenwood House

At the northern end of Hampstead Heath, this 1616 mansion was remodelled in the latter 18th century. Inside are beautiful period

interiors and a magnificent collection of paintings, including masterpieces by Rembrandt, Gainsborough and Vermeer. Outdoor lakeside concerts are held here in summer.

📍 Hampstead Heath ☎ 020 8348 1286 🕐 11.00–17.00 Apr–Oct, 11.00–16.00 Nov–Mar Ⓜ Hampstead

National Maritime Museum

This royal park was designed by John Nash. Britain's maritime history is explored in the extensive galleries of this historic building, which surround the glass-roofed Neptune Court. Rooms are devoted to the expeditions of great explorers, the life and battles of Admiral Nelson, trade and empire, luxury liners and naval art.

📍 Greenwich Park ☎ 020 8858 4422 🌐 www.nmm.ac.uk
🕐 10.00–17.00, until 18.00 July–Aug Ⓜ DLR Cutty Sark

Ranger's House

This Georgian villa literally became the Greenwich park ranger's house in 1815. Now it houses the art collection of Julius Wernher, who made his fortune in South African diamonds.

📍 Chesterfield Walk, Blackheath ☎ 020 8853 0035 🕐 10.00–17.00 Wed–Sun, Apr–Sept; admission charge Ⓜ DLR Cutty Sark

RETAIL THERAPY

Shopping Streets & Markets

Camden Market What began as a collection of bohemian stalls in 1972 has become London's busiest market, attracting over 150,000 shoppers every weekend. If you're claustrophobic, come early or late to browse the eclectic stalls running along Camden High Street, beside Camden Lock and up into Chalk Farm Road. The market hall has several floors of indoor shops. Some shops and stalls are open all week, but the market is busiest on weekends with four or five times as many stalls and much more happening. 🌐 www.camdenlock.net 🕐 09.30 or 10.00–17.30 or 18.30 🚇 Camden Town

Camden Passage Market The antiques market here is fun to browse, though you probably won't find any bargains. The surrounding antiques shops are open all week. 📍 Camden Passage, off Upper Street 🌐 www.camdenpassageislington.co.uk 🕐 07.00–14.00 Wed, 08.00–16.00 Sat 🚇 Angel

Greenwich Market The crafts and clothes at this large venue are a cut above your average inner-city market. Stalls in the covered Crafts Market sell antiques on Thursday and clothes, handicrafts and gifts Friday–Sunday. 📍 College Approach and Stockwell Street 🕐 07.30–17.00 Thur, 09.30–17.30 Fri–Sun 🚇 Greenwich train from Charing Cross or DLR Cutty Sark

TAKING A BREAK

Brew House £ ❶ The café set in the old laundry at Kenwood House serves breakfast and lunch, as well as a good selection of tea and cakes. There is outdoor seating on the terrace and in the courtyard. 📍 Hampstead Heath ☎ 020 8341 5384 🕐 09.00–18.00 🚇 Hampstead, Highgate

Camden Lock £ ❷ The weekend food stalls in West Yard at Camden Lock Market dish up huge helpings from a great range of exotic fare, with tables and chairs set out along the canal. 🚇 Camden Town

Goddard's £ ❸ Savoury pies and other traditional café fare is served at this tiled eatery near the *Cutty Sark*, which dates from 1890. ⓐ 45 Greenwich Church Street ⓣ 020 8692 3601 ⓛ 10.00–18.30 Mon–Fri, 10.00–19.30 Sat & Sun ⓝ DLR Cutty Sark

AFTER DARK

Restaurants
Trafalgar Tavern £ ❹ Charles Dickens drank here and used it in scenes from *Our Mutual Friend*. You can still enjoy the same great riverside views, whitebait and good pub meals. ⓐ 5 Park Row ⓣ 020 8858 2437 ⓛ 11.30–23.00 Mon–Sat, 12.00–22.30 Sun ⓝ DLR Cutty Sark

Jin Kichi ££ ❺ This Japanese restaurant is popular for its excellent food, which ranges from grilled skewers of meat or quail's eggs to sushi, but it's small and very busy so it's best to book ahead. ⓐ 73 Heath Street ⓣ 020 7794 6158 ⓛ 18.00–23.00 Tues–Fri, 12.30–14.00, 18.00–23.00 Sat, 12.30–14.00, 18.00–22.00 Sun ⓝ Hampstead

Pasha ££ ❻ Smart contemporary decor complements the delicious fresh fare at this Turkish restaurant, which serves authentic and sophisticated dishes. ⓐ 301 Upper Street ⓣ 020 7226 1454 ⓛ 12.00–15.00, 16.00–23.30 Mon–Thur, 12.00–15.00, 16.00–24.00 Fri & Sat, 12.00–23.00 Sun ⓝ Angel, Highbury & Islington

Cinemas & Theatres
Almeida Hollywood stars often appear in the cast of the classic revivals, new works and European plays produced here by top-notch directors. ⓐ Almeida Street, Islington ⓣ 020 7359 4404 ⓦ www.almeida.co.uk ⓝ Angel, Highbury & Islington

King's Head London's oldest and most highly regarded pub theatre. Lunchtime and evening productions range from classics to new playwrights to musicals. ⓐ 115 Upper Street, Islington ⓣ 020 7226 1916 ⓦ www.kingsheadtheatre.org ⓝ Angel, Highbury & Islington

Sadler's Wells Theatre This world-class dance venue presents the most stimulating productions in the capital, from modern dance to ballet and opera by British and international dance troupes. ⓐ Rosebery Avenue ⓣ 0870 737 7737 ⓦ www.sadlerswells.com ⓝ Angel

Bars, Clubs & Discos
Fabric Three great dance floors and fantastic music make this Clerkenwell club one of the highly rated in London. Queues are long so come early. ⓐ 77a Charterhouse Street ⓣ 020 7336 8898 ⓦ www.fabriclondon.com ⓛ 21.30–05.00 Fri, 22.00–07.00 Sat, 22.00–17.00 Sun ⓝ Farringdon

ⓞ *The Millennium Dome is easily recognisable for miles around*

Jazz Café Not only jazz, but R&B, soul, Latin, hip hop and more set the changing scene at this laid-back spot. There's a restaurant upstairs and a balcony overlooking the stage – book ahead for a good table.  5 Parkway, Camden  0870 150 0044 (box office)  www.jazzcafé.co.uk  Camden Town

Lock 17 This Camden venue on several levels incorporates two of London's best-known names for nightlife: the legendary Dingwalls which has been at the forefront of the live music scene for three decades with gigs Sunday through to Thursday, and the stand-up comedy club Jongleurs, which has one show on Friday nights and two on Saturdays.  11 East Yard, Camden Lock  020 7428 0010  www.dingwalls.com  www.jongleurs.com  www.lock17.com  Camden Town, Chalk Farm

Roundhouse This round brick building, built as a Victorian engine repair terminal and later a venue for top rockers in the 1960s and 1970s, reopened in 2006 after extensive renovation as a youth arts centre and dynamic new performance space for music, theatre, dance, circus and more.  Chalk Farm Road  0870 389 1846 (box office)  www.roundhouse.org.uk  Chalk Farm

Turnmills With a cool split-level dance floor and top DJs, this is one of London's most popular nightclubs, especially on Friday's Gallery house and trance night.  63b Clerkenwell Road  020 7250 3409  www.turnmills.com  21.00–02.00 Thur, 22.30–07.30 Fri, 22.00–06.00 Sat, 21.00–03.00 Sun  Farringdon

● *Pointing visitors in the right direction*

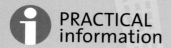

PRACTICAL
information

Directory

GETTING THERE

As Britain's capital city, connections to London are excellent for domestic, continental or international travel. No matter what mode of transport you choose, there are many options to fit all budgets.

By air

Domestic flights to London from cities around the UK have come down in price, particularly if you book well in advance, and are now a reasonable option for getting to London. It is generally cheaper to book online than through the airline or travel agent. Some airlines to try include:

bmi flies to London from Aberdeen, Belfast, Edinburgh, Glasgow, Leeds and Manchester. ☏ 0870 6070 555 ⓦ www.flybmi.com

British Airways has low-cost fares to London from Aberdeen, Edinburgh, Glasgow, Manchester and Newcastle. ☏ 0870 850 9850 ⓦ www.britishairways.com

easyJet flies to London from Aberdeen, Belfast, Edinburgh, Glasgow, Inverness and Newcastle. ☏ 0871 244 2366 (customer services; booking must be done online) ⓦ www.easyjet.com

Ryanair flies to London from Blackpool and Glasgow ☏ 0871 246 0000 ⓦ www.ryanair.com

These airlines also have low-cost flights to a variety of European cities. From Ireland, **Aer Lingus** ☏ 0818 365000

Ⓦ www.aerlingus.com has flights to London from Cork, Dublin and other cities.

Many airlines fly to London from North America. These include:
Air Canada Ⓣ 1-888-247-2262 Ⓦ www.aircanada.com
American Airlines Ⓣ 1-800-433-7300 Ⓦ www.aa.com
Continental Airlines Ⓣ 1-800-231-0856 Ⓦ www.continental.com

Many people are aware that air travel emits CO_2, which contributes to climate change. You may be interested in the possibility of lessening the environmental impact of your flight through the charity Climate Care, which offsets your CO_2 by funding environmental projects around the world. Visit www.climatecare.org

By rail

Rail travel is generally expensive, but you can sometimes get budget fares to London from other major cities around the UK if you are willing to book a week or longer in advance, and reserve specific trains and times. You will also get cheaper fares if you travel outside peak times. You can compare fares and may find some bargains if you book online. Two websites to try are Ⓦ www.thetrainline.com and Ⓦ www.qjump.co.uk

National Rail Enquiries is the place to contact for routes, timetables and other information across the entire national rail network.
Ⓣ 0845 748 4950 Ⓦ www.nationalrail.co.uk

Eurostar has services to London Waterloo from France (Ⓣ +(33) 08 92 35 35 39) and Belgium (Ⓣ +(32) 25 28 28 28) Ⓣ 08705 186 186
Ⓦ www.eurostar.com

By road

If you're driving from the continent, the most convenient way to reach London is via **Eurotunnel**, which runs the train service through the Channel Tunnel. Drivers and passengers remain in their cars for the 20-minute journey between Calais and Folkestone. From Folkestone, follow the M20 north (junction 11a); the drive to London takes about an hour and a half. ☎ 0870 535 3535
🔵 www.eurotunnel.com

If you're driving to London from elsewhere in the UK, be aware of the Congestion Charge (see page 53). Some approximate driving times to London from around Britain are: Birmingham 193 km (120 miles) (2 hrs 20 min); Cardiff 245 km (152 miles) (2 hrs 50 min); Edinburgh 665 km (413 miles) (7 hrs 30 min); Manchester 328 km (204 miles) (3 hrs 50 min).

By bus

Long-distance buses serve London from most European cities as well as domestic destinations. They arrive and depart from **Victoria Coach Station**. 🅰 164 Buckingham Palace Road ☎ 020 7730 3499 (telephone sales)
National Express is the main carrier for domestic and continental routes. ☎ 0870 580 8080 🔵 www.nationalexpress.com

Package deals

A combination flight-and-hotel package will often save you money over purchasing them separately. You can also buy packages that include tickets to a concert, theatre or dance production, or other special event. Some good websites to check out include:
🔵 www.lastminute.com 🔵 www.expedia.co.uk or
🔵 www.expedia.com 🔵 www.deckchair.com

ENTRY FORMALITIES
Visa requirements

Visitors from most European countries do not need a visa to enter Britain (exceptions include Albania, Bosnia, Bulgaria, Croatia, Macedonia, Montenegro, Romania and Serbia) and can stay for up to three months. Citizens from EU countries need only a valid passport and can stay indefinitely. Visitors from Canada, the United States, Australia and New Zealand do not need a visa and can stay for up to six months, as long as they have adequate funds and a return ticket.

Customs

Visitors to London from within the EU are entitled to bring their personal effects and goods for personal consumption and not for resale, which can be up to 800 cigarettes and 10 litres of spirits. Those entering the country from outside the EU may bring in 200 cigarettes (250 g tobacco, 50 cigars), 2 litres of non-sparkling wine and 1 litre of strong liqueur or 2 litres of sparkling wine or fortified wine, such as sherry or port.

TRAVEL INSURANCE

Visitors from other EU countries have reciprocal health schemes while in the UK. A European Health Insurance Card is now required to obtain health services. These reciprocal agreements may not cover all possible expenses, so it is advisable to take out a separate travel insurance policy. All non-EU travellers should ensure they have full medical insurance before they travel. Travel insurance policies that also cover lost or stolen possessions, flight cancellations, etc are highly recommended.

MONEY

The pound sterling (£) is Britain's official currency. £ = 100 pence (p). Notes are in denominations of £5, £10, £20 and £50. Coins are in denominations of 1p, 2p, 5p, 10p, 20p, 50p, £1 and £2.

The quickest and easiest way to obtain cash is by using an ATM, or cashpoint. They are widely found at airports, railway stations, in the city centre and on the high streets of greater London. Most cashpoints take a variety of cards, and a list of these is posted alongside the machine. Instructions are given in English and other major European languages.

Bureaux de change facilities can be found at the airports, at major railway stations, at the main high street banks and at many post offices. There are also facilities such as Chequepoint, which offer 24-hour money changing services in central London. The rates for cash and traveller's cheques and the commission rates should be clearly displayed. It pays to shop around, as rates vary. Banks generally offer higher rates.

Credit cards are widely accepted throughout London, though smaller cafés, shops and pubs may take cash only. Visa and MasterCard/Eurocard are most widely accepted, but most places accept American Express, Diners Club and others.

HEALTH, SAFETY & CRIME

No special health precautions are necessary when visiting London. Tap water is safe to drink (except in public toilets or if otherwise posted) and tastes fine; bottled water is also widely available.

Pharmacies (chemists) are labelled with a green cross. The largest chain is Boots and there is generally one on every high street. Many large supermarkets such as Tesco and Sainsbury's also have in-store pharmacies which may keep longer hours. Most chemists are open during normal business hours, and operate a rota system for after hours opening; these times are displayed in the shop window or the local newspaper. To find the nearest pharmacy, try these websites:

Boots the Chemist Ⓦ www.wellbeing.com
Superdrug Ⓦ www.superdrug.com
Lloyds Pharmacy Ⓦ www.lloydspharmacy.com

Healthcare in the UK is of a very high standard, and is provided by the National Health Service (NHS) as well as private physicians. Although doctors' visits are free to those with a European Health

🔺 *An open top bus tour will show you the major sights*

Insurance Card, there is a basic charge for prescriptions and other services. Visitors from outside the EU should expect to pay for consultation and services. Be sure to obtain a receipt in order to claim on your travel insurance policy.

Should you need medical assistance, your hotel should be able to help you to find the nearest doctor or facility. You can also use the website w www.nhs.uk/localnhsservices to find a doctor, dentist or chemist nearby. There are several NHS walk-in centres in central London. For non-urgent problems you can also contact NHS Direct to obtain medical advice from a qualified nurse over the phone t 0845 4647 or w www.nhsdirect.nhs.uk

London is generally a safe place, but as in all large cities you should be alert and take precautions. Petty theft is the main concern, rather than violent crime. Keep an eye on your valuables and keep wallets and handbags secure, especially on crowded trains and buses and in markets or other crowded places where pickpockets operate. Try not to sit in empty carriages on trains and the Tube, or on the upper decks of buses late at night. Always lock your car and never leave valuables inside.

Tourist areas in the city centre are generally safe after dark, but avoid unlit streets and passages. There are a few areas to steer clear of, so check with your hotel for advice. If you're out late, use a black cab or licensed minicab for a lift home.

Police constables wear dark blue uniforms and caps. Those who patrol the streets are very approachable and will give information and directions if needed. Transport police are on duty at railway stations and on the Underground.

For details of emergency numbers see the Emergencies section, page 154.

OPENING HOURS

Banks are open Monday–Friday 09.30–16.30, with some large branches also opening on Saturday morning. ATMs are available round the clock. Office hours for most businesses are 09.30–17.30.

Post office hours are normally Monday–Friday 09.00–17.30 and Saturday 09.00–12.00. Some sub-post offices close for lunch 13.00–14.00.

Normal shop opening hours are Monday–Saturday 09.00 or 09.30 to 17.00 or 17.30 but can vary widely. Department stores in central London remain open until 18.00 or 19.00, with late-night shopping one night a week (usually Thursday) until 20.00. Bookshops are often open until 22.00. Newsagents across London open from around 07.00 until around 20.00 and are also open on Sunday until around 15.00. Convenience stores are open late.

Museums and attractions are generally open Monday–Saturday 10.00–17.00 and Sunday 12.00–17.00, but hours vary. Many museums close one day a week, often Mondays. Last admission for many attractions, particularly large palaces, museums, etc. is one hour before closing time.

TOILETS

Your best bet for toilets in central London are the large department stores. Pubs around the city will generally let you use their facilities, though other bars and restaurants may expect you to purchase food or drink. Public toilets near subways and in train stations are best avoided except in large stations such as King's Cross, Liverpool Street and Victoria, where the 20p entry fee assures relatively clean facilities. Self-cleaning cubicles can also be found in some parks and squares.

CHILDREN

Many restaurants, pubs and hotels in London are child-friendly, while others have a 'no children' policy or only welcome children over a certain age. The larger chains are good for providing high chairs and child menus. If pubs admit children (those that do often have outdoor seating areas), they must be accompanied by an adult and under 14s are not allowed in the bar area.

Nappies, baby food and other necessities are widely available at pharmacies and supermarkets. Most public toilets have baby changing facilities in the women's toilet.

Children under 11 can travel free on the London Underground and Docklands Light Railway after 09.30 on weekdays and all day on weekends and public holidays, if accompanied by an adult. Bus and train travel is free to under-14s and to 15- and 16-year-olds with an Oyster photocard (see page 59).

Many of London's main attractions will appeal to children, including the Tower of London (see page 107), the Natural History

● *You're just an email away from home – internet cafés are plentiful*

Museum (see page 94) and the Science Museum (see page 94). Other good options include the following:

- **Bethnal Green Museum of Childhood** Adults will also be delighted by this East End museum with exhibits of toys, dolls and games spanning four centuries. There are children's activities and events at weekends. ⓐ Cambridge Heath Road ⓣ 020 8980 2415 ⓦ www.museumofchildhood.org.uk ⓛ 10.00–17.50 Sat–Thur ⓝ Bethnal Green

- **Diana, Princess of Wales Memorial Playground** With its Peter Pan theme, this adventure playground in Kensington Palace Gardens features a pirate ship, mermaid fountain, tree house and other attractions that appeal to children up to age 12. ⓛ 10.00–dusk ⓝ Queensway

- **Hamleys** The biggest toy store in London is a big draw for kids of all ages, with five floors of the latest games, dolls and gadgets. ⓐ 188–196 Regent Street ⓣ 0870 333 2455 ⓦ www.hamleys.co.uk ⓛ 10.00–20.00 Mon–Sat, 12.00–18.00 Sun ⓝ Oxford Circus

- **Little Angel Puppet Theatre** Shows at this charming puppet theatre in Islington range from marionettes to glove puppets. ⓐ 14 Dagmar Passage ⓣ 020 7226 1787 ⓦ www.littleangeltheatre.com ⓛ 11.00 and 14.00 Sat–Sun, phone for weekday shows; admission charge ⓝ Angel, Highbury & Islington

- **London Zoo** Set in Regent's Park, the zoo is perennially popular with children, especially the walk-through monkey forest,

penguin pool and live animal action shows. ☎ 020 7722 3333
ⓦ www.zsl.org/london-zoo ⏰ 10.00–17.30 Mar–Oct; 10.00–16.00
Nov–Feb; admission charge Ⓝ Regents Park

COMMUNICATIONS

Phones

Most of London's classic red phone boxes have been replaced by
modern silver ones, and are widely found around the city. Most
accept both coins and phone cards, but some accept credit cards
only. They take 10p, 20p, 50p and £1 coins, and sometimes £2 coins.
Only fully unused coins are returned if your call is short. Phone cards
can be purchased at newsagents and post offices in various
denominations, and a display will tell you how much credit is left.
The minimum charge for a local call is 20p. Calls to mobile phones
are much higher than land line calls.

Useful numbers

Directory enquiries are run by several competing services and you
will be charged for the call. They include BT 118500 and One.Tel 118111
For international directory enquiries try BT 118505 and One.Tel 118211
Operator ☎ 100
International operator ☎ 155

The city code for London is 020, followed by an 8-digit number.
You do not need to dial the city code within the city limits.

To telephone London from abroad, dial the international code
(011 from North America, 0011 from Australia, 00 from New Zealand)
plus the UK country code (44) plus the London city code minus the
initial zero (20) plus the 8-digit number.

To telephone abroad from the UK, dial 00 followed by the
following country code, area code (minus the first zero) and local

number. Country codes are listed in the phone directory and include:
Australia 61   **Canada** 1   **France** 33   **Germany** 49
Ireland 353   **New Zealand** 64   **USA** 1

Post

London is well served with a main post office in each area and numerous sub-post offices located in newsagents throughout the capital, so there is always one not far away. You can also buy stamps at newsagents. Post boxes are usually red and round and located on the high street, or a slot in the wall on the outside of post offices.

First class stamps within the UK cost 32p, second class 23p. Letters and postcards to Europe weighing up to 20 g cost 44p. To the rest of the world, letters and postcards weighing up to 10 g cost 50p and, up to 20 g, 72p.

Internet

Internet access is widely available through numerous internet cafés across the capital. A good central internet café is easyInternet Café ⊚ 354–358 Oxford Street ① 020 7241 9000 Ⓝ Bond Street. They also have branches in Kensington High Street, Trafalgar Square, Tottenham Court Road and the King's Road.

ELECTRICITY

The UK uses 240 volts AC current. Plugs have three square pins. If you are bringing appliances from a country where the voltage is different, you will need a converter and probably a plug adaptor as well.

TRAVELLERS WITH DISABILITIES

Newer hotels, restaurants and attractions have been adapted for people with disabilities, but older buildings may not have complete access. Call in advance to see what facilities are available. Some tube stations have lifts (elevators) to platforms but most do not and there can be a lot of stairs, escalators and long corridors in many stations. You can check an accessibility map on Ⓦ www.thetube.com, or call Ⓣ 020 7941 4600 during business hours or Ⓣ 020 7222 1234 all other times. Buses with low floors run on many routes throughout London and more are being introduced.

Facilities for visitors with disabilities arriving at London's main airports are good, and some trains and shuttle buses from the airports to the city centre are wheelchair accessible. At Heathrow, the Disabled Living Foundation has a Travelcare service and can offer advice Ⓣ 020 8745 7495, minicom Ⓣ 020 8745 7565.

Other useful contacts include:

Artsline can provide information on disabled access to arts attractions and entertainment events. Ⓐ 54 Chalton Street, NW1 1HS Ⓣ 020 7388 2227 Ⓦ www.artslineonline.com

Holiday Care Service can advise on suitable accommodation for disabled visitors Ⓣ 0845 124 997 Ⓦ www.holidaycare.org.uk Ⓗ helpline open 09.00–13.00 Mon–Fri

The Royal Association for Disability and Rehabilitation (RADAR) can also offer advice. Ⓐ 12 City Forum, 250 City Road, EC1V 8AF Ⓣ 020 7250 3222 Ⓦ www.radar.org.uk

TOURIST INFORMATION

London's official tourist information organisation is Visit London Ⓣ 020 7234 5888 Ⓦ www.visitlondon.com. In addition to the ones listed below, there are tourist information booths at Heathrow and

Gatwick airports and at Waterloo, Victoria and Liverpool Street railway stations.

Britain & London Visitor Centre ⓐ 1 Lower Regent Street ☎ 020 8846 9000 ⓦ www.visitbritain.com 🕒 09.30–18.30 Mon, 09.00–18.30 Tues–Fri, 09.00–17.00 Sat, 10.00–16.00 Sun, June–Sept; 09.30–18.30 Mon, 09.00–18.30 Tues–Fri, 10.00–16.00 Sat & Sun, Oct–May Ⓝ Piccadilly Circus

City of London Visitor Centre ⓐ St Paul's Churchyard ☎ 020 7332 1456 🕒 09.30–17.00 Mon–Fri Apr–Sept; 09.30–12.30 Oct–Mar

London Information Centre ⓐ Leicester Square ☎ 020 7292 2333 ⓦ www.londontown.com 🕒 08.00–23.00 Mon–Fri, 10.00–18.00 Sat & Sun Ⓝ Leicester Square

London Visitor Centre ⓐ Arrivals Hall, Waterloo station, International Terminal 🕒 08.30–22.30 Mon–Sat, 09.30–22.30 Sun

FURTHER READING

London: The Biography by Peter Ackroyd is a lively history of the city by one of its great historians. *The Clerkenwell Tales* and *Hawksmoor* are two of Ackroyd's novels set in the city.

Brick Lane by Monica Ali is a popular novel exploring life in multinational London, as is Zadie Smith's *White Teeth*.

There's no better place to read Charles Dickens. *Oliver Twist*, *Little Dorrit* and *Bleak House* are some of his popular novels set in London.

Emergencies

The numbers 999 or 112 are the nationwide numbers to call for emergencies requiring police, fire or ambulance services. The operator will ask you which service you need and where you are calling from.

MEDICAL SERVICES

You can use the website ⓦ www.nhs.uk/localnhsservices to find a doctor, dentist or chemist nearby. There are several NHS walk-in centres in central London. For non-urgent problems you can also contact NHS Direct to obtain medical advice from a qualified nurse over the phone. ❶ 0845 4647 ⓦ www.nhsdirect.nhs.uk

If you are in need of emergency dental treatment, contact the **Dental Emergency Care Service** at Guy's Hospital, ⓐ St Thomas Street, Bankside ❶ 020 7955 2186 🕐 09.00–17.00 Mon–Fri ⓝ London Bridge. Arrive early (no later than 11.00) if you want to see a dentist that day. They can also refer you to a dentist near you.

Several hospitals in central London have 24-hour Emergency Departments. These include:

Chelsea & Westminster Hospital ⓐ 369 Fulham Road, Chelsea SW10 ❶ 020 8746 8000 ⓝ South Kensington

Guy's Hospital ⓐ St Thomas Street, Bankside ❶ 020 7188 7188 ⓝ London Bridge

Royal London Hospital ⓐ Whitechapel Road, Whitechapel ❶ 020 7377 7000 ⓝ Whitechapel

St Mary's Hospital ⓐ Praed Street, Paddington ❶ 020 7886 6666 ⓝ Paddington

---

❿ *Some public phone boxes also allow you to text, email and surf the web*

University College Hospital ⓐ Grafton Way ⓣ 020 7387 9300
ⓝ Euston Square, Warren Street

POLICE

Police stations are listed in full in the phone directory. Those in central London include:

Charing Cross Police Station ⓐ Agar Street, Covent Garden
ⓣ 020 7240 1212 ⓝ Charing Cross
Marylebone Police Station ⓐ 1–9 Seymour Street
ⓣ 020 7486 1212 ⓝ Baker Street
West End Central Police Station ⓐ 27 Savile Row, Mayfair
ⓣ 020 7437 1212 ⓝ Piccadilly Circus

Lost Property

Lost property should be reported to your nearest police station, who will register the details and provide the necessary report for an insurance claim.

For lost or stolen credit cards, contact the bank or card company immediately. Some numbers are:

American Express ⓣ 01273 696933
MasterCard/Eurocard ⓣ 0800 964767
Switch ⓣ 0870 600 0459
Visa/Connect ⓣ 0800 895 082

For property lost on a plane, contact the relevant airline; if lost in the terminal, contact the airport for their lost-and-found department (see pages 48–52). Items lost on Tube trains or buses are generally turned in to the local police department, and then forwarded to the Transport for London Lost Property Office
ⓐ 200 Baker Street ⓣ 020 7918 2000 ⓦ www.tfl.gov.uk
ⓒ 08.30–16.00 Mon–Fri ⓝ Baker Street

Lost property forms are available at the Tube stations. You can also call ☎ 020 7222 1234 for the phone number of the bus depots on the relevant route.

CONSULATES & EMBASSIES

American Embassy ⓐ 24 Grosvenor Square ☎ 7499 9000
ⓦ www.usembassy.org.uk ⓝ Bond Street, Marble Arch

Australian High Commission ⓐ Australia House, Strand
☎ 020 7379 4334 ⓦ www.australia.org.uk ⓝ Holborn, Temple

Canadian High Commission ⓐ 38 Grosvenor Street ☎ 020 7258 6600
ⓦ www.canada.org.uk ⓝ Bond Street

Irish Embassy ⓐ 17 Grosvenor Place ☎ 020 7235 2171 ⓦ www.dfa.ie
ⓝ Hyde Park Corner

New Zealand High Commission ⓐ New Zealand House, 80 Haymarket
☎ 020 7930 8422 ⓦ www.nzembassy.com ⓝ Piccadilly Circus

South African High Commission ⓐ South Africa House, Trafalgar
Square ☎ 020 7451 7299 ⓦ www.southafricahouse.com
ⓝ Charing Cross

🔺 *Most attractions are well-signposted*

The publishers would like to thank Christopher Holt and Pictures Colour Library Ltd for supplying the copyright photos for this book.

Copy editor: Natasha Reed
Proofreader: Jenni Rainford-Hairsine

Send your thoughts to
books@thomascook.com

- **Found a great bar, club, shop or must-see sight that we don't feature?**

- **Like to tip us off about any information that needs updating?**

- **Want to tell us what you love about this handy little guidebook and more importantly how we can make it even handier?**

Then here's your chance to tell all! Send us ideas, discoveries and recommendations today and then look out for your valuable input in the next edition of this title. As an extra 'thank you' from Thomas Cook Publishing, you'll be automatically entered into our exciting monthly prize draw.

Send an email to the above address (stating the book's title) or write to: CitySpots Project Editor, Thomas Cook Publishing, PO Box 227, The Thomas Cook Business Park, Unit 18, Coningsby Road, Peterborough PE3 8SB, UK.